A QUIET ESCAPE

Moments to replenish your soul

Compiled and Edited by

Peggy Horn &
Lillian Sparks

A Quiet Escape
Moments to Replenish Your Soul
Compiled and Edited by Peggy Horn and Lillian Sparks

Printed in the United States of America
ISBN: 1-880689-11-1
Copyright 2004, Onward Books, Inc.

Cover design by Matt Key

The opinions contained herein do not necessarily represent the views of other participants.

*To my best friend, Ken, through sickness and in health.
You're the best. Also, to those ladies who made my
"kitchen" experiences memorable.*

Peggy Horn

*To all the women who influenced my life and
left their fingerprints on my heart—my junior class
Sunday School teacher; my youth leader; my friend,
Muriel; my dear sisters—Faith and Ruth, who have
always believed in me; and of course, my mom,
who taught me how to be like Jesus.*

Lillian Sparks

CONTENTS

FOREWORD

In recent years, our culture has gained a greater appreciation for the contributions women can make in every sector of society. The body of Christ discovered this long ago. In the New Testament, Jesus elevated the status and value of women. Today women are blazing trails in missions, evangelism, compassion ministries and more.

This volume is a compilation of devotions from women with a wide range of ministry experiences. They are pastors, pastors' wives, missionaries, evangelists, teachers and music ministers. These ladies minister in local churches and districts, in national and international ministries. They appear on television and radio, write books and magazine articles; they touch lives in a variety of ways.

All of the authors in this volume have proven ministries and understand the needs of the everyday life of a woman. These authors are all extraordinary and ordinary . . . just like every woman who will read this book. The editors of this book, Peggy Horn and Lillian Sparks, are also experienced in ministry and well-qualified to compile such a work.

If you are looking for a book that offers all the answers, this is not it. But if you are looking for one that is honest and forthright, one that plumbs the depths of life and shows how other women of faith have come to grips with the same kind of challenges you face, then this book is for you.

Though all of these women are involved in demanding and often highly visible ministries, they are not super-women. Their down-to-earth look at everyday life will strengthen your spirit. And readers who are wrestling with a lack of self-confidence will find their value highly affirmed. Women are assured they have a place . . . and challenged and assisted to find it.

These devotionals can be read a day at a time or any way in which you choose. In these chapters you will find a refreshing vulnerability that will inspire and sometimes surprise you. Many will bring a tear to your eye.

Each of the 36 chapters offers a theme Scripture and culminates in a four-part exercise that will help you make the lesson of the chapter your own. Moments to Reflect, Refresh, Refocus and Respond will help you apply the thoughts to your life.

I commend to you *A Quiet Escape: Moments to Replenish Your Soul.*

— Huldah Buntain
Missionary to India

ACKNOWLEDGMENTS

*Special thanks to Ken Horn,
Matt Key, Shirley Speer, Scott Harrup and Lucas Key.*

CHAPTER 1

Let Resurrection Live

$\diamond$

Bonnie Argue

I have stilled and quieted my soul.
Psalm 131:2 (NIV)

Labor Day, September 2, 1991, JR "met" Jesus.

Extended family had come to our home, but only our sons, Dru, Kent and Terry, were with me in the bedroom for a marvelously impacting, unforgettable moment. We prayed together. While kneeling at JR's bedside, Kent suddenly stretched his hands forward. Waving them above his father's body, he gasped, "He's going! He's going! He's *gone!*"

My pastor-husband, Watson Argue Jr., had been hospitalized with physical threats that seemed to have no definition. The death certificate did note that the immediate cause of death was lymphomatosis meningitis, which he had for only two weeks. At one point, our doctor walked me outside the hospital and apologized for misdiagnosing cells that had seeped into the spine, affecting nerves and limiting use of feet and hands. Almost to the end, JR preached from a wheelchair, but he could not hold his Bible.

After several memorial services, I recall being impressed in my spirit with these precise words: *Now, just rest! Just rest!* I stopped what I was doing and opened my NIV Bible to the instruction I needed. I read aloud, slowly:

"I have stilled and quieted my soul; like a weaned child with its mother" (Psalm 131:2).

"The fruit of righteousness will be peace; the effect of righteousness will be quietness and confidence forever" (Isaiah 32:17).

"He makes me lie down in green pastures, he leads me beside quiet waters" (Psalm 23:2).

"Be still before the Lord" (Psalm 37:7).

"Let the peace of Christ rule in your hearts" (Colossians 3:15).

The words *just rest* came to me over and over, even in that season of death. I would keep saying, "Bonnie, just rest! Just rest!"

Although Scripture tells about Joshua's shout at the walls of Jericho (Joshua 6:16,20) and about David's audible songs (1 Samuel 16:23), yet, somehow I would be reminded of the quiet confidence and rest that was present in the lions' den (Daniel 6) and with Shadrach, Meshach, and Abednego in the fiery furnace (Daniel 3).

Sensing those four words, *Just rest, just rest,* was of monumental importance in my burden-loaded prayers. Sometimes being still is a key to receiving help and for guarding our ears so we recognize the voice of God.

"Rest" in Hebrew is *damam*[1]. Notice the lips are closed, silent with the "mmmmmm." Resting is about being still, being quiet.

It was during this "rest" emphasis that I realized some ministry changes would bring relocation for me. Where does a widow go next? When do I sell the house? How do I blend with church leaders who request my counsel in selecting a new minister? *Just rest,* right?

Our Heavenly Father is so faithful as He guides us with His wisdom and righteous judgments.

Relevant events were clarified very soon. The new pastor was installed, and his ministry continues. But, now, where do I go? Again, Bonnie, *just rest.*

After several months, I received a call from Asia about taking the pastorate of Zoe Christian Fellowship, Ltd. in Hong Kong. I remained there with a strong congregation of hundreds of men and women who were employed as government and domestic workers. To accommodate holidays, we had eight services a week and I continued that schedule for eight years. Yes, I was at *rest.*

We can be confronted with various life plans and challenges—crushing experiences, death of family members, or loss of business ventures. This is where the spiritual disciplines and continual honoring of the Word of God bring a sacred map before us.

There will be sorrow, grief, or even death. But, being in Christ, we do not grieve as those who have no hope. I knew I could not continue the deep, private grieving and sorrow of loss of my life partner. It was during Easter when the message of resurrection again pierced my spirit with such reality. I prayed with an audible declaration, "Let resurrection live!" I became inspired and set myself to focus on the stories of Jesus' death and resurrection. This brought truth for my daily challenges.

Let the message of "Resurrection" inspire you today. Read this poem aloud and with emphasis. Be encouraged with God's plan and purpose for His chosen family!

Let Resurrection Live!

The festal trumpet air I hear in clear, distinct "hurrah"
Announcing earth's most glorious theme,
*   and heaven's coup d' etat.*
Exceeding, awesome power and might was mastered
*   when God gave*
To Jesus resurrection life and snatched Him from the grave.

*We celebrate this day each year with Easter togs and tams
And lily pots and sunrise throngs, and bunnies, eggs
  and hams.
The hymns that once each year we sing (like carols sung
  at Yule)
Are tucked away like Christmas balls. Who authorized
  that rule?*

*Now, listen, Church, our Lord's alive! Delight! Rejoice!
  Be glad!
Should we not make this Easter time the longest we have
  had?
For, tell me . . . Why should resurrection be but for a day,
When we all know this life in us has settled in to stay?*

*It's absolute . . . infallible . . . a documented creed
That I am truly raised in Christ, and Christ is raised indeed.
Each day I live in vital faith to demonstrate the fact
That resurrection life in me is more than just an act.*

*Let's understand our message: It's the resurrection way
With the Master Molecule within . . . our Father's DNA!
In Him I live in righteousness. God's Nature through me
  flows
In wisdom, pow'r ability . . . as each believer knows.*

*If Christmas causes us to share our gifts and cards and
food;*
Is Easter not a GREATER time for celebration mood?
*Oh, yes, it is! I shout the claim and challenge your
assent.*
*These gifts and cards and feastings grand are Easter's
fitting vent.*

So, resurrection people, *rally to the trumpet's sound.*
*Gather friends and kin for feasting; sing and laugh and
dance around.*
*Every day this year, be thankful for your "zoe"–powered
bod . . .*
Resurrection's *quick'ning vigor! Thank You, Jesus!
Thank You, God!*

—Bonnie Argue

MOMENTS TO REFLECT:

Do you see and recognize God's presence as you think
on this season of your life? Are you aware of His love
and desire to be involved? It's like gazing into a mirror
which brings truth and honesty before you.

MOMENTS TO REFRESH:

Enjoy the refreshing as you talk to God, as you pray
and even as you sing to the Lord. Cherish this experience. It's a daily necessity!

MOMENTS TO REFOCUS:

As we sorrow, thoughts and memories can quickly come that would cloud our calling, our vision and even the reality of the present. Don't embrace self-pity. Stay aware of your vertical relationship with the Lord. A new era is before you.

MOMENTS TO RESPOND:

Develop the habit of daily reading the Bible . . . aloud. Hear your lips quote, "Whoever believes on Him will not be put to shame" (Romans 10:11). Wear the Word and prove it as you move forward into His will, into His next chapter for your life.

Bonnie Argue is associate minister at Christian Life Church, Santa Rosa, California. Bonnie trained for ministry at Central Bible Institute in Springfield, Missouri. Upon graduation she and Watson Argue Jr. married and began ministry in Canada, the U.S. and the world.

Bonnie's extensive and varied ministry includes such highlights as directing the Seoul, South Korea, choir one Sunday during a ministry visit, at the invitation of Pastor David Yonggi Cho; financing the emergency room in the first Mark Buntain Hospital in Calcutta, India; having tea with Corrie ten Boom in her home; and visiting the Lillian Trasher Orphanage in Assiout, Egypt.

Contact Bonnie Argue at: bonnieargue@msn.com.

CHAPTER 2

Mountain-Moving Power

Mona Blackwood

Whoever says to this mountain, "Be removed and be cast into the sea," and does not doubt in his heart, but believes that those things he says will be done, he will have whatever he says.
Mark 11:23 (NKJV)
Read Mark 11:20-25

When we are faced with a great need, either for ourselves or for others, we should begin by humbly seeking to know God's will in the matter: "Father, what do You want to do in this situation?" Jesus said, "My Father has been working until now, and I have been working" (John 5:17). He listened to the voice of the Father, and He watched Him. Be careful not to pray passively, "If it be Your will," without first seeking to know God's will in the situation. Many prayers are weak because this step has been skipped. When He reveals His will to you, your prayer can be more specific. When God has witnessed to your heart that He wants to perform a miracle, you can then pray for that miracle with more energy and faith.

It is often important to exercise a key to the miraculous—the spoken word. God has given believers authority over disease, demons, sickness, storms, and finances (Matthew 10:1; Luke 10:19). Often, we keep asking God to act, when, in fact, He calls us to employ His authority by declaring in Jesus' name for an affliction to leave, for a crisis to end.

Jesus said, "Whoever says to this mountain, 'Be removed and be cast into the sea,' and does not doubt in his heart, but believes that those things he says will be done, he will have whatever he says" (Mark 11:23). Believe in your heart that it has already happened! With the anointing of faith that God gives you, speak it forth. But remember, miracles come by faith in God's present power, not by ritual or formula of human works or by willpower.

From Jesus' own lips we receive the most direct and practical instruction concerning our exercise of faith: (1) It is to be "in God" (Mark 11:22). Faith that speaks is first faith that seeks. The Almighty One is the Source and Ground of our faith and being. Faith only flows to Him because of the faithfulness that flows from Him. (2) Faith is not a trick performed with our lips, but a spoken expression that springs from the conviction of our hearts. Faith in our hearts is to be spoken, and thereby becomes active and effective toward specific results, as taught here by the

Lord Jesus. (3) Jesus' words "whatever things" apply this principle to every aspect of our lives. The only restrictions are (a) that our faith be "in God," our loving Father, and in alignment with His will and Word; and (b) that we "believe"—not doubting in our hearts (Mark 11:24). Thus, "speaking to the mountain" is not a vain or superstitious exercise or indulgence in mind-science, but instead an applied release of God's creative word of promise.

Our Savior's action in cursing the fig tree indicates a passion in prayer and faith that we need to learn (Mark 11:20,21). When the disciples later noticed with surprise that the tree had withered completely, Jesus responded with a sharp command, "Have faith in God." Then He said, "speak to mountains." He led them to prepare for situations in which they would find it necessary to take direct authority in the spiritual realm to impact things in the natural realm.

When you believe that God exists and that He loves you and wants to meet your needs, this creates faith in your heart. On the other hand, doubt is just as real. The reverse of faith, doubt tells you that God does not exist or that He is unloving and uncaring about your needs. Doubt gives rise to fear, which brings torment, not peace. Fear actually keeps you from receiving the good things God desires to send your way. Those who are double-minded, God says, will not receive anything (James 1:6-8).

Jesus goes on to say, "Whenever you stand praying, if you have anything against anyone, forgive him, that your Father in heaven may also forgive you" (Mark 11:25). A great hindrance to miracles is a lack of forgiveness. Whether or not the attitude is justified by the circumstances, there must be freedom from bitterness and resentment or there will be no mountain-moving miracles. There can be no resentment, no bitterness, no jealousy, no envy—none of these things. To see miracles, there must be forgiveness and love.

Capture this truth: Doubt, and do without; with faith believe, and receive.

Expect a miracle!

Expectancy opens your life to God and puts you in a position to receive salvation, joy, health, financial supply, or peace of mind—everything good your heart longs for, and more!

MOMENTS TO REFLECT:
Think of times you have doubted and times you have had faith. How did they differ?

MOMENTS TO REFRESH:
Realize that God is a loving Father whose desire is to bless you.

MOMENTS TO REFOCUS:
Focus on the great promise of Mark 11:23.

MOMENTS TO RESPOND:
Believe God's promises, then act on them by praying in faith and speaking to your mountain.

Mona Blackwood was born and raised in Tennessee. She is married to Jimmy Blackwood, award-winning former lead singer of the Blackwood Brothers Quartet and other groups. She has traveled in ministry both nationally and internationally. As office manager for Jimmy Blackwood Ministries, she coordinates the ministry and writes regularly for the ministry newsletter. Married for 40 years, Mona and Jimmy have two daughters and five grandchildren. They are members of Raleigh Assembly of God in Memphis.

Contact Mona Blackwood at: www.jimmyblackwood.org.

Hope in Time of Loss

Mary Jane Boggs

Therefore encourage each other with these words.
1 Thessalonians 4:18 (NIV)
Read 1 Thessalonians 4:13-18

For the second time in less than a month our family gathered together to make arrangements to bury a loved one. How could this have happened? Our grief was almost overwhelming and we all felt that we were too tired and weak to go through this ordeal again so soon. Such a loss, a loss that left us reeling with pain and heartache.

We were a large family, nine adult children with families of our own. In fact, there were 35 grandchildren and 35 great-grandchildren. Now we had just lost the two people who were the head of this "clan." My father loved all of us; every new baby was a welcome delight to him. No one could hold an infant and sing a lullaby like my mother. The grandchildren had all enjoyed their place in her arms and could sing the songs she loved so much. They were two very special people.

The death of my parents represented two types of loss. One was a gradual, creeping, sneaky thief known as Alzheimer's disease. The other was a sudden onslaught, an attack that came so close on the heels of the first that it left us numb to the bone. Now each of us had to learn to go on living without them. We adult children who always relied on our parents' advice and prayers were now the "older generation" and would have to fend for ourselves. We were adult orphans. The very word sounded cold and harsh. And we couldn't cope with the truth of it.

First, let me emphasize that both parents were devout Christians. They had served the Lord since before their wedding 62 years ago. They had graduated from high school together, and married shortly afterwards, choosing to use a class ring for a wedding band. On their 25th anniversary, my father's gift was a set of real wedding and engagement rings. My mother wore them with pride for the rest of her life. We children knew they loved each other with all their hearts. Even Christmas in our home ran a close second to their anniversary date.

Mother was the first to leave us. Surrounded by a few close family members, we watched as she slipped away into the presence of the Lord. We sang "Amazing Grace" and prayed together, and just as if she were waiting for the end of the prayer, she took her last breath immediately following the "Amen." The disease that had taken away her strength and even her recognition of her family could not take away the love of music and prayer. The Holy Spirit was with her and with us as we gave her a farewell kiss on the forehead and began to make the necessary final arrangements.

My dad was in control, or seemed to be. He knew what had to be done and how he wanted it done—the music, the ministers, the spot in the family cemetery, and who should be notified of her death. We merely tried to follow his wishes and support him with our prayers and our presence. Little did we know that in just a few days he would also be gone. The stroke he suffered was massive and he only lived for 12 more hours. The doctor said he died from a broken heart. We found ourselves once again making calls and planning a memorial service.

How did we cope with it all? We turned to the source of our strength, God's Word, and allowed the Holy Spirit to comfort us. Just as our mother had held us as children, we leaned on Him and just sobbed our hearts out because we knew that our Heavenly Father understood our sorrow. Our great High Priest, Jesus Christ, our Intercessor, was ready and willing to allow us to grieve for our loss and then give us strength to go on living with our memories.

We comforted ourselves with the promises we found in the Word. King David, upon hearing about the death of his son, knew that he could not bring him back from the dead, but that he could go to him (2 Samuel 12:22,23). We knew this also applied to the loss of our parents, therefore we promised ourselves that we would live the kind of life that would be pleasing to God and would not bring shame to the testimony of our loved ones. We had been taught to trust in the Lord with all our hearts; we would not betray that trust now in our time of sorrow.

We comforted ourselves in knowing that our parents were in the presence of the Lord. Neither one of them would have wanted to stay on this earth without the other. We knew we would see them again someday. We knew we were allowed to have our time of mourning; we also knew we were not mourning as those who have no hope.

At both memorial services, the minister read Psalm 116:15, "Precious in the sight of the Lord is the death of his saints." We felt this to be a confirmation that God was present with us and our parents were present with Him. We continue to live with that hope and trust in Him.

MOMENTS TO REFLECT:

Read Psalm 23 and remind yourself that death is only a shadow, and shadows, unlike walls, can be passed through.

MOMENTS TO REFRESH:

Read Revelation 21:4 and rejoice that there will be no tears in heaven.

MOMENTS TO REFOCUS:

Read Isaiah 55:12,13 and Psalm 30 and allow yourself to experience the joy of the Lord which He can give after a time of sorrow. "Weeping may remain for a night, but rejoicing comes in the morning" (Psalm 30:5).

MOMENTS TO RESPOND:

Read Psalm 78:1-7 and ask yourself if the next generation will know about God's love and provision because
you were faithful to share the good news with them.
Ask the Lord to give you opportunities to leave a legacy
of hope despite the hard times.

*Mary Jane Boggs is an ordained minister with the
Kentucky District of the Assemblies of God and has served
as the district Women's Ministries director for 28 years.
She and her husband, Isaac Troy Boggs, have pastored several Assemblies of God churches in Kentucky.*

*Mary Jane is a graduate of Marshall University in
Huntington, West Virginia, and did two years of post-
graduate work at Eastern Kentucky University. She has
been a librarian and teacher in public schools and also
spent five years as director of a Christian school. She is
now employed part-time as a substitute teacher.*

*Mary Jane is the mother of four children: Violet Sue,
Rose Mary, David Isaac, and James Allen. She and her
husband have 10 grandchildren and 10 great-grandchildren. They live in London, Kentucky.*

Contact Mary Jane at: boggs.mary@ramcell.net.

CHAPTER 4

Survival Kit for Hard Times

Anoosh Markosian Bullock

Can a mother forget the baby at her breast and have no compassion on the child she has borne? Though she may forget, I will not forget you! See, I have engraved you on the palms of my hands.
Isaiah 49:15,16 (NIV)

I arrived in America from the former communist Soviet Union in 1977. I remember my first visit to a grocery store. I had never seen so many aisles loaded with goodies, and to my great surprise nobody was standing in line to buy bread. I saw chicken already plucked, cleaned, and nicely packed, hamburger already ground, stew meat cut in bite sizes, and different flavors of ice cream. I felt like falling on my knees to praise God. My memory went back to my own country . . . how I could go to the store and count everything on the shelves on my two hands. And how at times I had to fast and pray for basic needs such as butter, potatoes, cotton balls, size 10 white shoes and dark brown stockings to match my dress. But God always provided my needs (Philippians 4:19).

Even in the U.S., nobody can guarantee that you will never face hardship, heartaches, struggles and disappointments. Life is loaded with unpredictable twists and turns and sometimes the course of life can change radically. John 16:33 says, "In this world you will have trouble. But take heart! I have overcome the world." The same God who overcame the world lives inside you and me and He is able to bring us through victoriously, no matter how big our challenges are. Even when you cannot sense His presence He is still with you, causing everything to work out for good (Romans 8:28). Nothing touches our lives that is not sifted through the hands of God. Present trials may be instruments of blessing down the road. I have personally experienced disappointments that were God's appointments. Not only my steps, but my stops are ordered by God.

Perhaps you find yourself facing a dire predicament. Perhaps you are asking, how can I survive in these hard times? No matter what you are going through, let me share this good news:

God has not forgotten you. One of Satan's favorite lies is that God has forgotten you. Satan reminds you of the sin you committed 10 years ago or your lack of reading the Bible and praying enough. But no matter what you are going through, God has not forgotten you. God knows when you sit down and stand up (Psalm 139:2). He has engraved your name on the palm of His hand because you are valuable in

His sight. Even when it appears that God is distant, He is still near. We do not walk by sight but in the reality of His promise that He will never leave or forsake us.

I praise God that He did not forget this little girl when I used to go and kneel on the floor of my bathroom and pray, read His Word, and rejoice over His promises such as "all things are possible with God" (Mark 10:27) and "Jesus Christ is the same yesterday and today and forever" (Hebrews 13:8). I remember praying, "God, since American missionaries have made such a great impact in my life, someday I would love to be the wife of an American minister and touch the world with the gospel of Jesus Christ." In the eyes of the world that was an impossible dream, since nobody was allowed to leave my country. But we serve a God who is awesome and mighty, who easily breaks the laws of nature. In 1976 God answered that prayer. I married an American youth pastor, Alan Bullock, in a seventh-century Orthodox church in Soviet Armenia. Now we are touching the world with the gospel of Jesus Christ.

The source of your help is God, not people. Put your trust in God. People change, their memories fade, their abilities and strength weaken. But God never changes. He does, however, change things.

In your hard times first run to God in prayer. "The prayer of a righteous man is powerful and effective" (James 5:16). You don't have to impress God with fancy words. He understands.

Second, feed your mind with the Word of God. It will give you hope and encouragement. It will lift your spirit. It will turn your fears into faith. That is why Satan fears your discovery of God's Word; ignorance of it is a powerful weapon he can use against you.

When I came to America, I went to a Christian bookstore. I stood at the foot of a clearance table. I could not believe what I saw—a Bible on sale for 97 cents. I fought back tears. I remembered how my pastor during the time of communism copied the Bible by hand. I remembered tearing pages from my Christian books to share with other believers. Every time I read my Bible today I say, "Thank You, God, for allowing me to have my own personal Bible."

Endure hardship unto the Lord. Second Timothy 2:3 says, "Endure hardship with us like a good soldier of Christ Jesus." Many of us manage to endure but not without complaints.

Choose to endure gratefully, not grudgingly. James 1:2,3 says, "Consider it pure joy, my brothers, whenever you face trials of many kinds, because you know that the testing of your faith develops perseverance." Philippians 4:4 says, "Rejoice in the Lord *always*. I will say it again: Rejoice!" When you train your tongue to praise God regardless of your circumstance it takes your eyes off your problem and focuses on the great problem solver, Jesus Christ. If the apostle Paul could rejoice in the dark, damp, dirty and stuffy prison in Rome, then I can adjust my attitude and train my tongue to rejoice in the Lord and be content in every situation.

We are all temporary residents of this world. Our eternal home is in heaven. The storms we now face will not last. In the meantime, let us work for Him with a grateful attitude. Let us live with our eyes focused on the end of the journey, when He will say, "Welcome, My faithful servant."

MOMENTS TO REFLECT:
While you are waiting for your prayers to be answered, make your waiting room into a worship room and your prison into a praise room.

MOMENTS TO REFRESH:
God will not let us go through more than we can handle. Our Master knows our limit.

MOMENTS TO REFOCUS:
Let us not put limitations on God's ability. When He acts, everything has to get out of His way.

MOMENTS TO RESPOND:
"I will bless the Lord at *all* times: his praise *shall* continually *be* in my mouth" (Psalm 34:1, KJV).

Anoosh Markosian Bullock was born in Iran to an Armenian Christian family. When her family moved to the Soviet Union, she became active in the underground church.

In 1976, Anoosh graduated from a university in the Soviet Union with a B.A. in linguistics. Since her arrival in America in 1977, Anoosh has served as a foreign language instructor in the Defense Language Institute in Carmel,

California. She has also taught physical education in California and Florida. She has worked in Southern California and Alabama Teen Challenge centers, where her husband, Alan, served as executive director. She has served as Women's Teen Challenge director in Orlando, Florida. She has written and translated praise and worship songs into Armenian. Anoosh travels across America and abroad, speaking in churches, missions conventions, retreats, and at various other Christian events.

Anoosh's brother-in-law, the general superintendent of the Assemblies of God in Iran, died a martyr's death. Anoosh reminds her audiences not to take their many freedoms for granted.

Anoosh and Alan have appeared on several television and radio programs, including The 700 Club, Daystar Television Network, and Trinity Broadcasting Network. The Bullocks have two children and reside in North Texas.

Contact Anoosh Markosian Bullock at: anooshusa@aol.com.

But I Only Have So Much Time

Leslie Callaway

Jesus, tired as he was from the journey,
sat down by the well.
John 4:6 (NIV)
Read John 4:1-42

One hundred sixty-eight hours, that is all we get, every week. Great people have figured out how to turn that limited amount of time (that we all get) into service that inspires others to become more than they were before.

The words "Somebody ought to do something about that" are an opportunity to have the abundant life that Jesus promises (John 10:10). Jesus was about one primary thing—gently leading individuals toward their potential. That is our calling, and that is the only way we reach our potential and get what God has for us.

In speaking to women across this country, as I am introducing the hospitality ministry of Mon Ami to churches, women's groups and leadership meetings, I have asked them what their needs and desires are. The responses are consistent—time, isolation, seeing the purpose of a ministry involvement, and personal enrichment.

Jesus, the Author and Perfector of our faith (meaning the one whose actions direct ours if we follow Him), dealt with time, isolation, seeing purpose and was enriched personally all in the same time frame that we have. He touched the life of a woman and impacted a community for God. Interestingly, He did all that while on the way to somewhere else. He saw a need (a person) and *took* the time to offer a breath of life. When I look back at some of the times when God used me most effectively, they were times when I was "on the way to somewhere else." Jesus was really on His way from Judea to Galilee to begin some of His most fruitful times of ministry. Rarely is God's timing ours, or His ways our ways (Isaiah 55:8,9).

Jesus was in a hurry—Scripture declares, "He had to go through Samaria" (John 4:4). He did not have the time to go around Samaria like any self-respecting Jew *always* did. As far as the Jewish people were concerned, walking through Samaria was walking through a sewer. But His schedule did not allow Him the time that everyone else seemed to have. Jesus had to deal with those same scheduling frustrations that you and I so often have. I love serving a God who knows.

In the midst of that hurry, Jesus was impressed to stop right in the middle of Samaria—the wrong place. Why is it that the stop signs of our lives always seem to be in the wrong places? But the same God who set the timing for the universe sets the timing for the events of our lives. God's divine purpose was about to be clarified in a strange and uncomfortable way.

Jesus, a preacher, a model of morality, was sitting at a well needing a drink of water. Who came along—one of the well-respected ladies of the community, or a member of the local Women's Ministries? Of course not. Who showed up to get water but the woman with the worst reputation in the village. She was there in the middle of the day, because she knew that she dare not come to the well when respectable ladies come in the evening and the morning to get water. Jesus could have thought, *Oh great . . . tired, hungry and time pressed, and now this. Just look busy, and she will move on.*

This woman knew isolation, rejection and distrust. That was her life. Earned, probably. She was a threat, real or perceived, to every woman who had a husband in that village. She had had her chance, and she had blown it. She had no friends. Around town, the looks that she got, whether "Hey, baby" or "What are you doing here," said the same thing—you are not worth much, if anything.

Imagine the woman's shock when this well-known preacher even spoke to her. Jesus had eyes directed by the Holy Spirit that saw a woman not necessarily bound to her lifestyle. He saw worth where no one else did. Others' opinions were not going to determine His. That same Holy Spirit that directed His vision can direct ours. After all, when we were apart from God, were we really any different in God's eyes (see Romans 3:10,23)? Faith sees reality before others do. Nowhere is faith more needed than in our "eyes" when it comes to seeing worth that others do not see. Through this, Jesus breathed life back into a woman.

But our lives demand one more question—WWJG (What Would Jesus Get?). What did He get for His trouble? God made us reward-oriented. Heaven and hell are the number one motivation system in creation. Malachi 3:10-12 is nothing if not a divinely inspired incentive program. What did Jesus get? Scripture declares that the whole village came out to see Him due to her testimony. We do not know what a "respectable person" could have achieved, but she evangelized the entire town. Holy Spirit-inspired vision, seeing the "person" that others see as an object, achieved Jesus' goals effectively and efficiently— the village came to Him. In addition, when He was offered food later, He did not need it. He had stopped because He could not go on. He gave what others were unwilling to give, and He was refreshed without the normal expense associated with it. What do I get out of reaching out? Much more than you could anticipate. That is a promise signed by God.

God has given us gifts packaged as hassles. All it takes is a lady to take some of that 168 hours and seek Holy Spirit eyes to see what others have missed—a person of great worth. Just like Jesus and someone else saw in us.

MOMENTS TO REFLECT:
How am I really looking at person(s) whom I could easily dismiss as not my type?

MOMENTS TO REFRESH:
God values people, not schedules. Being a Christian means seeing people (especially that person who is easily ignored), not the clock.

MOMENTS TO REFOCUS:
Potentially wonderful relationships begin with moving beyond our comfort to reach someone others have avoided.

MOMENTS TO RESPOND:
Seek God to have "eyes to see" and pour life into some lonely person's life, then *begin* the answer to that prayer.

Leslie Callaway is a sought-after speaker and the founder of Mon Ami Ministries. For years Leslie spent countless hours counseling women in need due to loneliness and other relationship concerns. Her goal of giving women a sense of being loved by providing a time of care and elegance led Leslie to found Mon Ami in the fall of 2001. Since her beginning the ministry with a basket, a tea set and a heart to serve, Mon Ami has been implemented in nearly every state and has reached beyond this continent.

For more than 20 years Leslie has been active in ministry to children, youth, and women, as well as in music ministry. *She is an award-winning singer and songwriter. She teaches speech-level voice. Leslie speaks for women's groups and regional conferences across the country.*

Leslie is the wife of Rev. Mark L. Callaway, a pastor and attorney. She is the mother of Nathan and Shannon.

Contact Leslie Callaway (or for information on Mon Ami Ministries) at: callaway@nwiis.com.

CHAPTER 6

What Is It?

Debbie Calvert

I will rain down bread from heaven for you.
Exodus 16:4 (NIV)

Two months after the Israelites left Egypt and were freed from slavery, they found themselves in a desert, discouraged and hungry, complaining among each other and before their leaders, Moses and Aaron. God heard their grumbling and said to Moses, "I will rain down bread from heaven for you." So, in faith, Moses and Aaron went and told the people of God's soon-coming provision (Exodus 16:1-9).

As Aaron was speaking to the Israelite community, looking toward the desert, the glory of the Lord appeared in a cloud to Moses saying, "I have heard the grumbling of the Israelites. Tell them, 'At twilight you will eat meat, and in the morning you will be filled with bread. Then you will know that I am the Lord your God.' That evening quail came and covered the camp, and in the morning there was a layer of dew around the camp. When the dew was gone, thin flakes like frost on the ground appeared on the desert floor. When the Israelites saw it, they said to each other, 'What is it?' For they did not know what it was. Moses said to them, 'It is the bread the Lord has given you to eat'" (Exodus 16:12-15).

I wish I could say I was so mature in my faith that I am always appreciative of God's daily provision. Honestly, in my inconsistencies, I many times find myself feeling as one in a desert, alone and wondering where God is, much less seeing His provisions. In these times, I, too, become like my ancestors, the Children of Israel. Seeing how God put up with their sinful complaining and ungratefulness gives me hope of God's divine compassion and continued provision, even to this ungrateful child.

The truth is that our God still provides bread from heaven since "Jesus Christ is the same yesterday and today and forever" (Hebrews 13:8). Whatever our need, or perhaps complaint, He wants to hear it and be our provision. Because of our frail humanity, He realizes our need to be reassured that He is still the Lord our God, the One who has cared for us in the past, who cares for us now and who will do so in the future.

When they saw the bread, the Israelites said, "What is it?" Although God already told them He was providing bread, they had a hard time seeing the process of the provision, how the flakes mixed with the dew could ever make bread.

Isn't that like us? We know what God has promised and yet we stand looking at our situation, wondering. We, too, ask, "What is it?" In our endeavor for immediate bread, we lose focus on what God is doing and choose to focus on what is not done. Our gaze requires eyes of faith, a realization that it might not look like it yet, but it's the mixings of the promised provision, which, if we watch long enough, will manifest into bread, satisfying our hunger and fulfilling every hope and dream, becoming our everything.

Just as the flakes needed time to mix with the morning dew, those things God is preparing for us who love Him take time. In my personal experiences, often impatient, I have turned away in disappointment, losing focus on the promised provision, frustrating the divine plan. Upon arriving in Indianapolis several years ago, I sensed God speaking to my heart that it would be a preparation time in my life—preparation for the ministry God was calling me to. This season would require solitude, times of prayer and study, at home with God and my pet goldfish. Deciding that God and my goldfish were not enough, in disobedience, I took an office manager position. I was with people, enjoying a paycheck but so far from God's plan.

Six months later, I resigned, exhausted and spent, and decided to go back to solitude and finish my book manuscript that had been sitting dormant for eight years. Upon finishing the book, instead of marketing the book and working on my ministerial studies, I took a job doing some marketing for a local fast-food chain. It was part-time, but I learned the hard way that it was not God's divine plan for me to sell chicken! Three months later I resigned only to pick up another part-time position which lasted for another three months. Here's what I learned. Until we return to

God and ask, "What is it?" and remember daily His answer, "It's bread from heaven," we won't be content to be still and watch God's plan unfold.

Like the Children of Israel, our trust in God's provision often falters. For that we're truly sorry, and He is truly faithful to forgive. In regaining focus, we become convinced that bread is truly raining down from heaven, a fresh batch each day. God is waiting to see what we will do with it; and what we do with it will depend on how we choose to see it.

MOMENTS TO REFLECT:

"Because of the Lord's great love we are not consumed, for his compassions never fail. They are new every morning; great is your faithfulness. I say to myself, 'The Lord is my portion; therefore I will wait for him'" (Lamentations 3:22-24).

MOMENTS TO REFRESH:

"Keep falsehood and lies far from me; give me neither poverty nor riches, but give me only my daily bread" (Proverbs 30:8). Just as He did for the Israelites, He will give you exactly what you need just for today. Leftovers won't be necessary as new bread is promised for tomorrow.

MOMENTS TO REFOCUS:

Realize how much He loves you, even through your deepest struggles, doubts, disappointments, and, yes, even complaints.

MOMENTS TO RESPOND:

No more asking, "What is it?" Instead, look up and say with joy, "It's bread from heaven!"

Debbie Calvert is an author and motivational speaker, ministering at various meetings and conferences on the issues of spiritual and emotional freedom, challenging others toward their highest potential through God's Word. She is currently a recommended speaker for the national Women's Ministries Department of the Assemblies of God.

She has served on various Women's Ministries local and district boards for more than 15 years and has been active in children's, youth, music, jail, juvenile, and prison ministries.

Debbie and husband Bob have been married since 1982 and they have been in full-time pastoral ministry since 1983. They have two boys, Clay and Cody, still at home. She enjoys walks, fishing, and attending various sporting and music events with her family. She loves shopping with her husband, target shooting with a .357 magnum, watching football and golf, Putt-Putt, reading, writing and poetry.

Contact Debbie Calvert (or for information about her book, Out of Control: Just as He Likes Me!*) at: focusedonreallife@hotmail.com.*

CHAPTER 7

Rest for the Weary

Nancy Cawston

*Come to me, all you who are weary and burdened, and I
will give you rest. Take my yoke upon you and learn
from me, for I am gentle and humble in heart,
and you will find rest for your souls.*
Matthew 11:28,29 (NIV)

With an exasperated sigh, 5-year-old Loree slumped
over the kitchen table and moaned, "I'm just *de-zausted!*"
I comforted her with hugs and kisses, but didn't correct her
pronunciation. In fact, her word became a family expression. When we were totally worn out, we would say, "I'm
just *de-zausted!*"

Are you there today? Are you exhausted, not only physically, mentally, and emotionally, but spiritually as well?

You've been walking by faith, growing in discipline, serving others, fighting against evil—but you're worn out. I'm talking about the kind of weariness that a good night's sleep or a weekend getaway doesn't cure. It's the deep fatigue that Jesus related to when He said, "Come to me, all you who are weary and burdened." What is spiritual exhaustion? What causes it?

DISCIPLINE: Sometimes we get worn out fighting against our own sinful nature. Just when we think we have conquered a weakness, it rears its ugly head again. Discipline is exhausting! Jesus said the remedy for this kind of fatigue is, "Take my yoke upon you and learn from me." Imagine a calf yoked to an old ox to plough. The young animal bellows and drags his heels in the mud, but the ox just plods on. Finally the calf learns to walk in step, and the yoke feels lighter. It works the same way for us. Spiritual discipline is necessary, but it will never be easy until we quit struggling. God will enable us to change, but that growth will only happen when we fall in step with Him.

WARFARE: Sometimes we get weary fighting the enemy! Obstacles seem insurmountable, sin is on the rampage, friends and family members are far from God, there is increasing opposition to our leadership . . . and we get worn out. Eleazar, one of King David's mighty men, fought in fierce hand-to-hand combat so long that his hand "froze" to the sword. Are you there? You're still fighting, but you need new strength to finish the battle. Look at the end of the story, "The Lord brought about a great victory that day" (2 Samuel 23:10). We need to see that the battle is the Lord's! Let Him pry your paralyzed fingers off the situation, and watch Him win the battle for you.

ENDURANCE: It's tough to be in a long "holding pattern" waiting for the answer to prayer. We look for signs that the situation is beginning to change, then we are devastated when things turn for the worse. We will lose heart looking for signs. We have to keep our eyes focused on Jesus. Every great Christian has endured long periods of waiting. If we are required to wait, there's a valuable purpose in the waiting time. To survive, we have to learn how to live daily in God's strength.

SERVICE: Luke tells of Jesus visiting the home of Mary and Martha. Mary was sitting at Jesus' feet, absorbing His teaching, but Martha was rushing around preparing a meal. Martha got tired of Mary's "laziness" and said, "Lord, don't you care that my sister has left me to do the work by myself? Tell her to help me!" (Luke 10:40). Martha hit burnout! She felt unappreciated, and things weren't fair. So many serving jobs are thankless, unnoticed and taken for granted. The only way we can serve without losing heart is to do the "one thing" that Jesus said was needed, that is to sit at His feet, pour our frustration out to Him, and let Him comfort us. The comfort doesn't come instantly—we have to wait until our souls calm down, and our spirits grow quiet. But the comfort comes!

Discipline, warfare, endurance, and service are all necessary endeavors. However, when we are exhausted, we tend to fall into the trap of discouragement and self-pity. In that state of mind, we can easily give up and quit. The other temptation is to slide into a dull and dutiful existence. We may even resort to the latest spiritual fad or a frenzy of ministry activity to pump up our Christian experience. Either extreme will lead us to a spiritual dead end.[1] What is the cure for spiritual fatigue? Where can we find the strength and hope that we so desperately need?

GOD HIMSELF: Charles Swindoll says, "The Lord doesn't promise to give us something to *take* so we can handle our weary moments. He promises us *himself*. That is all. And that is enough."[2] The invitation of Jesus is "Come to Me." There are no quick answers, no five-step methods, no clichés—just himself. In exchange for our spiritual exhaustion, He will give us himself. Set aside some quiet time and draw near to God. Drink deeply of His love and strength. Be at rest!

A NEW PERSPECTIVE: Isaiah 40:31 says, "But those who hope in the Lord will renew their strength. They will soar on wings like eagles." God wants to give us a new perspective, but how can we soar like eagles when we're flat on our faces with exhaustion? The wings that lift us are praise and worship offered even when we are in difficult circumstances. Like the eagle rising on the very winds that could crush him against the cliff, we set our wings and rise into hope and joy. From that perspective, everything looks different.

The story is told of a little crippled girl whose father came home with a large birthday gift for her mother. The girl begged to carry the package upstairs to Mommy, but her father, thinking of her disability, said, "Honey, you can't."

His daughter said, "Yes, Daddy, I can. Please give me the package."

Reluctantly the father placed the gift in her arms, and then she smiled and said, "I'll carry the gift, and now Daddy, you carry me."

Dear friend, be encouraged today. Let God carry you when your strength is gone. Let Him give you fresh hope and a new perspective. It's always too soon to give up, and the potential for God's miracles is too fantastic to shuffle through your days.

MOMENTS TO REFLECT:

Have you become spiritually weary in any of the following areas: discipline, warfare, endurance, service?

MOMENTS TO REFRESH:

In your own words, describe what Matthew 11:28,29 says about the sources of renewed strength.

MOMENTS TO REFOCUS:

What are the dangers of discouragement and self-pity?

MOMENTS TO RESPOND:

Plan for an extended time alone with God. Take your Bible and journal. Write in your journal about the "rest for your soul" and the fresh perspective you discover.

Nancy Cawston is a pastor's wife from Bensalem, Pennsylvania, where she and her husband, David, pastor Christian Life Center. Nancy is a retreat and seminar speaker and teaches regularly for Bible study classes and women's meetings. The Cawstons have also pastored Bethel Church in San Jose, California, and First Assembly of God in Puyallup, Washington. They were also missionaries in Hong Kong, pastoring the International Christian

Assembly, and in the Netherlands where Nancy directed the choir of the Central Pentecostal Bible School.

Nancy is a graduate of Central Bible College. She also served as pianist for Revivaltime, *the Assemblies of God's national radio broadcast, for three years. She is the mother of three children and has seven grandchildren. From her rich background, Nancy encourages people in applying God's truths to practical life experiences, and finding the fulfillment promised to each believer.*

Contact Nancy Cawston at: ncawston@comcast.net.

CHAPTER 8

Adam and Eve—Married by God

Mary Ann Cole

Then the Lord God made a woman
from the rib he had taken out of the man,
and he brought her to the man.
Genesis 2:22 (NIV)

As the "golden" day drew near marking 50 years of marriage for my husband and me, many thoughts surfaced about our life together. A desire arose to review the institution of marriage as designed by God—specifically when I read the words "Adam and Eve were married by God."[1] Yes, God led Eve, His creation, to Adam and presented her to him. She was the last of God's created works, putting an honor upon her as the glory of man. She is a "crown to her husband," according to Matthew Henry. She was not created until everything was in readiness, such as a home, provision for her maintenance and a husband longing for her coming.[2] What an arrangement! Indeed, Adam and Eve were married by God.

As Eve was presented to Adam, he received her (Genesis 2:23), then said these familiar words: "Therefore shall a man leave his father and his mother, and shall cleave unto his wife: and they shall be one flesh" (Genesis 2:24, KJV).

According to Webster's Dictionary, "cleave" means to adhere, or to cling fast. Starting life together, Adam and Eve had everything going for them. An ideal arrangement. Yet even under ideal circumstances things go wrong when we disobey God. How often we follow our first parents.

Looking back, my husband and I didn't have everything in readiness, as was the case in Eden. However, we were united in spirit with a goal to be used in God's service. Being united in Christ is essential. The little home church was the sanctuary for our vows. It seemed fitting to make sacred and lifetime vows before God, the pastor, our family and witnesses in this special place.

It was serious business indeed. This was a covenant we were making (see Proverbs 2:17, NIV). Walking the aisle on my father's arm, strong feelings rushed over me. Excitement, joy, happiness, apprehension—all flooding in at once. Thankfully, there was the faith that God had led us to the wedding altar and we were trusting in His blessing to be upon our union. Genesis 1:28 reads, speaking of Adam and Eve, "God blessed them."

How tragic that cohabiting couples miss out on the most important element in marriage, God's blessings. Absent is the serious, solid commitment that says, "I will leave and cleave . . . this is for life, God helping me."

Recently the "Scene" section of our local newspaper featured an article on a young couple entitled, "Cohabitation Nation."[3] The couple had been living together for six years, recently became engaged and plan to marry in four years. The full page-and-a-half article gave their story, along with photos and statistics that described clearly the speed of the moral decline in our society, although that was not the intent. Without respect for God or His Word, people do what is right in their own eyes. It is shocking and saddening to the believer.

How comforting to have an omnipotent, all-knowing, ever-present Father God who shows us how to live orderly and confident lives. He is our source in every season of life. The early years of marriage often bring multiple moves and changes in location, employment, or vocation—all of which could be totally unexpected. At such a time, a couple must leave father and mother and cling fast to each other.

Becoming parents is an incredible highlight, a thrill and a blessing. A new life is entrusted to our care and nurture. Major adjustments come with this blessing. Couples are stretched to the limit and must mature quickly. The miracle of a new life coming to novice parents should cause us to trust God and cling to one another. At this stage of marriage, we must share responsibilities and give up our comforts. Then follows the training stage. How quickly this new little person walks, talks and challenges authority.

Clinging fast to God and to each other in the decisions of discipline is vital. This unity brings stability, respect and peace to the home. God's blessing will be evident.

Christian married couples have a secret weapon against the world and the enemy when they cling fast to God and to each other. There is no greater joy or reward than that which comes with faithfulness. Marriage is not without its challenges. Life's pathway may have hills and valleys, twists and turns. Plans may go awry. But God never changes. He is true to His Word. There will come a day of reaping the rewards of God's blessings because of a lifetime commitment to Him and to each other.

God's Word encourages us to "let love and faithfulness never leave you; bind them around your neck, write them on the tablet of your heart" (Proverbs 3:3). A poem by that familiar author "unknown" says it well:

Marriage is a promise to communicate and share,
To treat each other with respect, to listen and to care.
Marriage is commitment by a husband and a wife,
To be each other's lover, friend and confidant for life.

MOMENTS TO REFLECT:
God instituted marriage between a man and a woman and His blessing is upon that institution.

MOMENTS TO REFRESH:
A woman is her husband's glory (1 Corinthians 11:7) and she is of worth to him.

MOMENTS TO REFOCUS:

God is the best maker of marriages, therefore I can trust Him with mine.

MOMENTS TO RESPOND:

Lord, help me to cleave, adhere, and cling fast to You first and to my husband next so that Your blessing may rest upon us.

Mary Ann Cole is a wife, mother of two ordained Assemblies of God ministers, and grandmother of seven. She has served in ministry with her husband, Glen, for 48 years as a Bible teacher, accompanist and director of Women's Ministries. Presently she is serving as chairperson of the Ministry Wives Committee for the Northern California/Nevada District Council of the Assemblies of God of which her husband is the superintendent. Her hobbies are reading, music and creating memory books for family members, particularly each grandchild as they reach graduation from high school.

CHAPTER 9

Fear and Faith

Janet Creps

I can do everything through him who gives me strength.
Philippians 4:13 (NIV)

Towering waves surrounded him as the violent wind swept across the sea. There Peter stood with no support, nothing under his feet to keep him from sinking. *What was I thinking?* he wondered. *How could I have been so naïve to believe that I could actually walk on water? Am I crazy?* As he looked down, he was overcome by the threatening power of the wind and the sea that seemed to want to devour him. Then, helplessly, he felt terror rise with the mounting waves and his body began to sink.

Is fear a sin? Some Christians think so. However, being afraid can also have advantages. Fear protects us from life-threatening dangers that surround our daily existence. More importantly, apprehension is a normal part of our emotional makeup. Most people have been in situations where they have felt intense anxiety. Experiences such as flying, public speaking, or going to the dentist are common forms of distress outside our comfort zones.

Like Peter, many biblical heroes understood what it meant to step out into the unknown. Like all of us, they were only human.

For instance, the Old Testament relates the journey of Moses who became leery of God's call to lead the Israelites out from captivity in Egypt. As with Moses, God often sends His people into ventures that require them to traverse unfamiliar territory. Perhaps you are facing a similar challenge today and can relate to what Moses must have felt in the desert.

The prospect of stepping out into the unknown leaves us with two choices. First, we have the option of saying no. Moses insisted that he was not eloquent enough to lead the people into the Promised Land. His feeling of inadequacy is understandable. Moses was not being entirely unreasonable when he asked God, "What if they do not believe me or listen to me?" Perhaps you have told yourself that there are so many others more capable than you; or, you may feel the pressure to avoid the unfamiliar, and with it, the risk of failure. These forms of fear can make saying "no" seem like the only thing to do.

A few years ago I faced one of the greatest challenges of my life when I had an opportunity to do graduate study at the Assemblies of God Theological Seminary. I experienced the "too complex." I felt I was too old, had too little biblical education, and thought graduate school might be too hard for me. Saying "no" seemed logical, but thank God I said "yes"!

Our second option is to persevere. We can either remain in our comfort zone, shackled to our fear of failure, or we can take on the task at hand and be willing to be scared for a while. There is no middle place between fear and boredom in the drama of spiritual growth. The alternative to "being scared for God" is being bored and futile, not living the extraordinary, Spirit-filled life to which God has called us.

Feeling full of faith and power is only one part of being brave. The other part happens when we step out in faith even when we feel afraid. Despite my apprehensions, I began graduate school by taking just one class. My first day brought mixed feelings. I found the classroom experience frightening, but at the same time I was overwhelmed by the grace of God that opened this door of opportunity.

My first class led to taking more courses, and eventually to a degree program. Often God is not asking us to walk on water; He is just waiting for us to take the first step. Challenges provide the opportunity for that step to happen.

Like Moses, Peter had the courage to step out into the unfamiliar. In order to walk toward Jesus, Peter took the risk of sinking. Similarly, God is calling us to take risks while depending on Him. It is important to note that walking in faith isn't the same as bungee jumping. Faith isn't acting carelessly or failing to use common sense. Nor is faith an excuse to not be held accountable for our decisions. One cannot understate the importance of seeking God's wisdom, relying on support from your spouse, family and/or those to whom you are accountable.

Authentic faith focuses on God's abilities instead of one's own inadequacies. Great men and women of God are not necessarily the most spiritual or the most self-confident. They are ordinary people who lead extraordinary lives because they obeyed God by displaying immense courage even when they were afraid.

The Scriptures reveal that we are to work out our salvation with fear and trembling. Paul understood this truth clearly, saying to the Corinthian church, "I came to you in weakness and fear, and with much trembling. My message and my preaching were not with wise and persuasive words, but with a demonstration of the Spirit's power" (1 Corinthians 2:3,4). Many people whom the Holy Spirit uses to accomplish great works do so with shaky feet and stammering lips.

The choice is ours. We can take a chance and risk failing or we can narrow our risks by never stepping out of the boat. Perhaps you are at a crossroads where you need to decide whether or not to take a step of faith. Often past disappointments and failures stand in the way of experiencing God's greatest blessings. You may not always get it right. But God does not require us to be perfect. He is just asking for our obedience.

Scripture says that "I can do everything through him who gives me strength." The strength God gives us is much bigger than our mistakes, our fears, and our apprehensions. You *can* take that scary first step into the unfamiliar, even if you are trembling, because Christ has already walked there.

MOMENTS TO REFLECT:

What has God called me to do?

MOMENTS TO REFRESH:

Authentic faith happens when we focus on God's abilities instead of our own inadequacies.

MOMENTS TO REFOCUS:

Remember that "I can do everything through him who gives me strength" (Philippians 4:13).

MOMENTS TO RESPOND:

The greatest choice that we will ever face is whether or not we will believe God.

Janet Creps is a native of Wisconsin, and a musician and professional artist by background. She and her husband, Earl, have pastored three churches. Janet has traveled extensively as a speaker for women's, marriage, and college student conferences and retreats. In 2004 she completed a master of divinity degree at the Assemblies of God Theological Seminary. Janet and her husband reside in Missouri.

Contact Janet Creps at: jcreps2@juno.com.

CHAPTER 10

Embracing the Moment

Pamela Crosby

*There is "a time to embrace, and a time to refrain
from embracing."*
Ecclesiastes 3:5 (NKJV)

When I was a little girl I dreamed of all that life would surely hold. I would have the greatest vacations, the best marriage, and the most adorable children. I just knew that we would play together in a field of daisies and the house would never get dirty. It has been said that what lies between reality and expectations . . . is stress.

I would love it if life were more predictable, if our plans flowed together in the pattern we visualized. But the pattern is seldom cut to our expectations.

A man's life cycle follows a linear pattern. I don't need to remind ladies that we don't have a cycle nearly as predictable. We are more familiar with the peaks of stability and the depths of instability. Just look at the emotional changes in one month, then consider the cycles of a lifetime. Between wanting to meet needs around us and mundane tasks, a battle rages within.

Women have a challenge: How to meet the needs around us and yet maintain our own self-identity. The quest of the female heart is to find out how to remain whole . . . in every kind of "whether." "Whether" or not the job is overwhelming. "Whether" or not the husband's paycheck can meet life's demands. "Whether" or not the kids are screaming. "Whether" or not life matches up to your little-girl dreams. I thought I had a pretty good handle on that concept until I received a phone call.

"Mrs. Crosby, your test has come back positive."

Gasp!

"Are you OK, Mrs. Crosby?"

While fighting back tears: "Yes."

"Congratulations, Mrs. Crosby"

"Uh . . . thank . . . you."

Baby number four was on her way. Not what I expected. I cried like someone had died. I took it as the death of my dreams, my wants, my ways. I remember saying to my husband, "Honey, have you ever felt like God has taken over the steering wheel in the car of life? Well, I think He's not only behind the wheel, but He just pushed me out of the car!"

Little Kandace Grace was born—our little blonde beauty with a sparkle in her eyes. I would go through the daily routine of washing mounds of laundry, clearing mounds of dishes, and cooking mounds of food. There was little time for me, and when there was, I would just sit and wonder what happened to my well-thought-out life.

I felt something deep inside snap. I wasn't suicidal, but I didn't want to live anymore. For 10 months I lived with that silent pain. Oh, I learned how to put on the "smiley face" for the sake of my husband's ministry, all the while losing ground. My desperate prayer was like the Psalmist's, "Do not be silent to me, lest, if You *are* silent to me, I become like those who go down to the pit" (Psalm 28:1). I was losing the ability to think clearly and care for my family.

Marcel Proust said, "The real act of discovery consists not in finding new lands but in seeing with new eyes." The apostle Paul, once blinded by the Lord, prayed that the Ephesians would experience such a change of view: "I pray also that the eyes of your heart may be enlightened in order that you may know the hope to which he has called you" (Ephesians 1:18, NIV).

I continued to read the Word and pray, yet felt nothing. One morning I read Genesis 18, where God promises Abraham that Sarah would give birth to a son. Her reaction? "She laughed." The Lord said, "Why did Sarah laugh and say, 'Will I really have a child, now that I am old?' Is anything too hard for the Lord?"

Sarah lied and said, "I did not laugh."

"Yes, you did laugh," God replied.

Those words struck a chord in my submerged soul. You could almost hear Sarah saying, "Great, I follow my husband to an unknown land and this is what I get for being faithful and obedient? Now, when I am old and haggard, You make me this promise. Where were You when I was ready?"

And the Lord said, "Pam, you too have laughed at My promises." My mind reeled. *Never! When?*

He gently responded, "I have blessed you with a wonderful husband, but you laugh and wonder if he will ever change to fit your mold. I have blessed you with four beautiful kids and you complain about all the work they create for you. I have blessed you with promises fulfilled, and you always want for more. You have laughed."

I began to weep. Not just tears of "I'm caught," but tears of shame, sorrow, and remorse. In repentance I cried to the Lord, "I promise to embrace Your love in my life, no matter where it takes me."

The Lord strongly impressed on my heart, *I know you love Me. Yet you want My will on your terms. Pamela, you need to embrace the moments I give you and live them out in joy and acceptance. Every moment of your life is from My hand.*

Embrace the moments. That awesome thought enveloped me. God allowed a change of heart for Sarah. Could my heart change as Sarah's did?

In the Hebrews 11 "Hall of Faith," you'll find my twin, Sarah! The name Sarai means "contentious one." But God gave her "new eyes to see," and a new name, Sarah

(Genesis 17:15), which means "my princess." That means there's hope.

Kandace has become the delight of our home. She is a great reminder to me that when I can only see a snapshot of my life, God has a huge portrait view.

God desires to give His daughters "new eyes." It happens when we are "transformed by the renewing of your [our] mind[s]" (Romans 12:2). Normajean Hinders puts it in a nutshell: "Accept that this moment has poignancy and that pain, discomfort, disequilibria, can be my [your] tutor." We no longer see from the same perspective. The challenge is to let go of the controls and of our expectations and to fully take hold of what God has given us, a moment to embrace. Embrace every moment, as God intended.

MOMENTS TO REFLECT:

Pinpoint a difficult moment that you have experienced in life. What did you learn about yourself? What did you learn about God's faithfulness through it?

MOMENTS TO REFRESH:

Identify an unfulfilled dream or expectation that is causing unnecessary stress in your life. Ask God what He wants you to do with that dream or expectation.

MOMENTS TO REFOCUS:

Write two new disciplines that you believe would help bring peace to your mind and transform your attitudes (e.g., memorizing Scripture, playing worship music when stressed, etc.).

MOMENTS TO RESPOND:

Next time you come upon a moment of conflict, or an unfulfilled expectation, remind yourself you will never have the privilege to live this moment again. If this moment is from the hand of a loving Father, He must have something beautiful in store that your physical eyes cannot see. This would be a great time to memorize Ephesians 1:18.

*Pamela Crosby is the wife of Robert Crosby, pastor of Mount Hope Christian Center in Burlington, Massachusetts (a northwest suburb of Boston), and a mother of four children: Kristin, Kara, Rob, and Kandace. Pamela grew up in the Assemblies of God with her pastor-parents David and Shirley Krist. She has a great desire to see women discover their spiritual gifts, and find active roles in the Kingdom. Robert and Pamela have ministered in New York, Ohio, and New England where they have pastored for nearly 12 years. As graduates of Southeastern College, Pamela and her husband have co-authored books for couples and parents (*Creative Conversation Starters *published by Focus on the Family/Honor), and minister together at marriage retreats and special couples events. As an active pastor's wife, she speaks to women at conferences and events and has developed creative communication tools, theater ministries for all ages, and outreaches.*

Contact Pamela Crosby at: pcrosby@mounthope.org or www.mounthope.org.

CHAPTER 11

Your Dream Is Doable— Just Pay Your Do's

Kristy Dykes

*For the vision is yet for an appointed time; but at the end
it will speak, and it will not lie. Though it tarries, wait
for it; because it will surely come.*
Habakkuk 2:3 (NKJV)

When Catherine Marshall was a young woman, she was
diagnosed with tuberculosis. The treatment was enforced
bed rest 24 hours a day. She wrote in *To Live Again*, "This
period turned into a time of soul-searching to evaluate the
meaning of human life in general, and mine in particular."

She came across a book that spoke of the value of probing "to find one's precise dream—'the soul's sincere desires.'" In her journal, she wrote her own "soul's sincere desire": "To become a writer who will make a real contribution to my generation and to the world."

I believe that within every heart is a dream—the soul's sincere desire. I define dream as "a God-ordained desire" because I believe that as we are walking in His will, He places desires within our hearts that He wants to bring to fruition. That's an exciting thought!

A few years ago, my dream was to see my Christian fiction published. I had written more than 500 published articles and had worked for two *New York Times* subsidiaries, but I yearned to see my fiction stories published. I believe in Christian fiction. It's my feeling that if people can watch TV or participate in various hobbies, they can also read Christian fiction. It's not only entertaining, it's beneficial. Charles Colson said, "Stories change us because as we read, we identify with characters who demonstrate courage and self-sacrifice, and in the process our own character is shaped." Most importantly, Matthew 13:34 says, "Jesus used stories when he spoke to the people. In fact, he did not tell them anything without using stories" (CEV).

But this dream of mine, this "vision," as Habakkuk refers to it, seemed to be taking a long time, and I was weary of waiting. I felt like I was wrestling an alligator. Being a native Floridian, as are generations of my forbears, I've seen live alligators all my life. At one Florida attraction, a man (a brave one) wrestles an alligator. The gator throws the man (now "terror-stricken") to the ground, and they flail about as the audience winces and gasps for long, tense minutes. Finally, when it looks as if the man won't win, he does, and we all ooh and ah. With the gator now conquered, the wrestler pries apart its jaws and sticks his head in to prove his victory. During my quest to see my fiction published, I often felt like an alligator wrestler. It was hard and frustrating.

One day, my dream became reality. Amazingly, the editor entitled the book *American Dream*. It hit the CBA bestseller list and went into four printings with over 50,000 copies in print. I have now sold a total of five titles of Christian fiction (*American Dream, Sweet Liberty, Church in the Wildwood, The Tender Heart,* and *Room at the Inn*), and I'm working on many more.

I love to pray for people that their dream will come true. What is your dream? Whatever it is, it's doable—if you'll pay your "do's":

Do everything you know to do and do it diligently. Ecclesiastes 9:10 says, "Whatever your hand finds to do, do it with your might" (NKJV). Even though I had a degree in mass communications/journalism and had taught at two colleges, I went back to college and took fiction-writing classes for four years. For a total of seven years I studied the craft, devouring fiction technique books by the armloads and analyzing about 200 novels. I mastered dialogue mechanics, scene development, POV (point of view), show vs. tell, GMC (goals, motivation, and conflict), and more.

Do rest in the call. First Thessalonians 5:24 says, "He who calls you is faithful, who also will do it." I had to deal with doubts—would my dream ever come about? I had to endure rejections from publishers (what I later learned is common for writers). I said, "Lord, surely I can do something easier than this, like becoming a brain surgeon." A frequent prayer was, "Our Father, who art in heaven, and who also hath written a book . . . help!" I had to rest in my call and believe that God would bring it about. Someone said, "People don't fail; they quit," and I made up my mind I was not going to quit.

Do not want "it" above the Lord. Matthew 6:33 says, "Seek first the kingdom of God and His righteousness, and all these things shall be added to you." I put the Lord first, above my dream.

I ask you again: What is your dream? What is your soul's sincere desire, as Catherine Marshall referred to it? Catherine Marshall became one of America's most notable and best-selling Christian writers. The *New York Times* called her "America's most inspirational author." More than 25 million copies of her books are in print, and her novel *Christy* is estimated to have been read by 30 million people. A few years ago, the Christian publishing industry created the Christy Awards, named after Catherine Marshall's book, and it honors Christian novels of excellence each year. What is the longing down in your heart—your God-ordained desire? Whatever it is, it's doable—if you'll pay your do's!

MOMENTS TO REFLECT:

Waiting for anything is hard. Waiting on God isn't easy either. What are some specific things you can do to show you are placing your trust in Him?

MOMENTS TO REFRESH:

The neat thing about your God-given dream is that it will come true, as Habakkuk tells us. God's duty is to bring it about. Our duty is to wait for Him and not get ahead of God.

MOMENTS TO REFOCUS:

While waiting, we must do all we can. It's like that old saying "God will do His part as long as we do our part." What are some things you can do while you are waiting for Him to fully develop your gifts and talents?

MOMENTS TO RESPOND:

"Lord, I trust You to work out Your will in my life and to bring to fruition the dream of my heart. Father, once You develop this in me, help me to use it to bless others. In Jesus' name, amen."

*A native of Florida, **Kristy Dykes** is an award-winning author, speaker, and former newspaper columnist. She's taught at many conferences and two colleges, and she enjoys speaking for women's events. She serves on the Publications Advisory Board of* Woman's Touch *magazine and has written 600 published articles for many publications including two* New York Times *subsidiaries,* Guideposts Angels, *etc. She's proud to say she's a Christian* fiction author, and she enjoys helping new writers.

Kristy's favorite speaking topic is "How to Love Your Husband," based on Titus 2:4. She's zigzagged the nation delivering this message. Through her speaking, she desires to see women experience the powerful presence of Jesus.

Contact Kristy Dykes (or for information regarding her books) at: kristydykes@aol.com.

CHAPTER 12

Developing Confidence

Rosalyn R. Goodall

"For I know the plans I have for you," declares the Lord,
"plans to prosper you and not to harm you, plans to
give you hope and a future."
Jeremiah 29:11 (NIV)

As women, we are accustomed to being servants and people pleasers. But sometimes we may feel out of control in our eagerness to please, and that's when we become vulnerable. Satan would love to rob us of our purpose, our energy, and our joy. Depending on our personality and weaknesses, he can often be effective using one of the following seven strategies.

DISCOURAGEMENT

Sometimes women feel like failures, especially when we compare ourselves with others. Our life may not run as smoothly as someone else's. We may question our walk with God, and wonder if He will ever give us victories. During times of discouragement, "Take captive every thought to make it obedient to Christ" (2 Corinthians 10:5). Trust God and know that "the steps of a *good* man [or woman] are ordered by the Lord" (Psalm 37:23, KJV). Memorize God's promises that especially apply to what you're going through. Put them on index cards and hang them on your mirror, or carry them in your purse or planner and review them frequently.

OVER-COMMITMENT, STRESS, AND BURNOUT

This is a huge area, and Satan loves to find the woman who wants to serve God with all of her heart but can't say "no" to anyone or anything. She is on call 24 hours a day, seven days a week. That lifestyle often leads to stress and burnout. At that time a woman may feel sick, guilty, exhausted, or question her motivations . . . and maybe her salvation. Jesus didn't minister like that. He set a balanced example by taking time to rest and pray. He didn't die from overwork! Remember, you are the Lord's and He will handle your problems with you.

DESTRUCTION OF YOUR MARRIAGE AND FAMILY UNITY

There is power when you and your husband agree in prayer. If Satan can drive a wedge between the two of you, or keep you from discovering the prayer power you have together, he can make you weak and vulnerable.

You need to be one with your spouse emotionally. Respect your spouse and have open lines of communication with him. Date each other. Have fun together—personal fun, not just ministry. Take care of issues that keep you apart emotionally. Go to a counselor, if necessary.

Your children's needs are also important. It is critical that you listen to them and respect and encourage them. Don't place on them unreasonable or impossible demands for perfection.

UNREAL EXPECTATIONS

We will not meet everybody's expectations all of the time . . . no matter what we do, or how we do it. There will be times of fatigue and frustration, and, "The fear of man brings a snare" (Proverbs 29:25, NKJV). Honestly assess what you feel passionate about—what ignites your creative spark—and do the things you are gifted to do. It is exhausting trying to use our lesser gifts for the majority of our time. Be who you are gifted to be, since your ultimate responsibility is to please God.

WOUNDED FEELINGS

It hurts to be criticized, rejected, and opposed. The pain we feel is sometimes followed by anger, bitterness, and unforgiveness. We personalize criticism and rejection, and may resent people for hurting our husband or children. It may take a long time to realize what or who is behind these attacks. Remember, we fight not "against flesh and blood" (Ephesians 6:12). We must pray, "Lord, put Your hedge of protection around our hearts and our children's hearts and help us deal with each situation with wisdom and love." Claim the promise in Isaiah 54:17, "No weapon forged against you will prevail" (NIV).

DEPRESSION AND WORRY

Depression and worry are not from God, and when they go unhealed Satan has a foothold in our lives. Take responsibility for your life. Don't blame others, or feel sorry for yourself.

People with depression often feel they will never get over it. They are exhausted and can't sleep at night. Depression may be biochemical, so medication and counseling may be necessary. No matter how bad your life may seem, with God's help you can turn it into something better. Avoiding disappointment means avoiding life; disappointment is a necessary teacher.

PRIDE

We must also keep our egos in check. It is sad when Christians take credit for what God has done in their lives. Avoid the self-righteousness that comes when we measure ourselves against others and tell God that we are thankful we are not like others (Luke 18:11). One lady may be leading a Bible study, and another is just as much in God's will while doing dishes and talking to Him. All of the people we come into contact with are part of God's assignment for us. Be humble and ask God where you may have offended someone. Be quick to ask for forgiveness.

Be a yielded vessel, because you are an integral part of God's plan for your world. Take every opportunity to be yourself and to keep growing in the Lord!

MOMENTS TO REFLECT:

Which of Satan's seven strategies has he used against you?

MOMENTS TO REFRESH:

Realize that God has made you with a unique personality and set of abilities. He wants you to be yourself and use the gifts He has given you.

MOMENTS TO REFOCUS:

Focus on the positive alternatives to the seven strategies and how you can implement them in your life.

MOMENTS TO RESPOND:

Pray through each of the seven areas, committing yourself to the godly alternative in each, and asking God for help where you are most vulnerable.

Rosalyn R. Goodall has served as a pastor's wife, missionary in Vienna, Austria, and instructor of business communication and English at Southwest Missouri State University. She and her husband, Wayde, pastor First Assembly in Winston-Salem, North Carolina. They have two children.

Contact Rosalyn Goodall at:
RGoodall@firstassembly-ws.org.

CHAPTER 13

What Do You Have in Your House?

A Shepherd's Staff, a Boy's Lunch, and a Bit of Oil

Denise Goulet

How can I help you? Tell me, what do you have in your house?
2 Kings 4:2 (NIV)

When God is about to do a miracle in our lives, He generally uses something we already have, something He has already provided us with. Regardless of the circumstances, He causes us to draw from within to find strength, power and peace.

In the fourth chapter of Exodus, when Moses asked how he could get the people to listen to him and to believe he truly had heard from God, the Lord answered him with a question: "What is that in your hand?" (v. 2).

"A staff," said Moses. Then God began to show Moses how He was going to use that simple, ordinary staff to do amazing miracles; miracles that would convince all but the hardest of hearts; miracles that, thousands of years later, are still capable of filling us with awe.

Another example can be found in the sixth chapter of Mark, where Jesus told His disciples to do something that, to them, seemed impossible. He wanted them to feed a crowd of more than 5,000. When they wondered aloud how they were to do this, He answered them with a question: "How many loaves do you have?"

They said, "Five—and two fish" (v. 38). Then the Lord took that small amount of simple, ordinary food—barely enough to feed one hungry little peasant boy—and, after giving thanks for it, began to divide it up and serve it. He didn't stop until the whole crowd had been served. Mark goes on to tell us that everyone ate and was satisfied—and there were 12 basketfuls of broken pieces of bread and fish left over.

My favorite is the story of Elisha and the impoverished widow. She came to the prophet one day with a devastating set of circumstances. Her husband, a God-fearing man and a prophet, had died leaving her in debt and with no way to pay back the money. So, as was the practice in those days, the creditor was going to take her two sons to be his slaves.

Now, this woman could hardly have been needier or more helpless. She must have exhausted all of her resources. We are not told why she had lost everything. We do not even have a hint why other family members could not rescue her from her distress.

Imagine the storm of emotions she must have been going through. Still grieving the loss of her husband, she was probably filled with pain and loneliness. Perhaps you can relate to this level of crisis. My husband and I can. As parents we have had to face asthma, seizures, rebellion, accidents and cancer. In the ministry we have faced death threats, rejection, gossip, financial battles and even an attack on our campus. I will never forget the weeks following the completion of our church sanctuary that seats 3,000. We discovered that our eldest daughter had cancer, my father-in-law contracted a fatal form of cancer, then the attacks started within the church and outside the church. It was a year that the grace and presence of God became so real. My husband often prayed during this time, "Lord, as we are getting squeezed on every side may the wine that comes out be sweet."

Pain and tragedy have a way of making you feel like you've got nothing. The woman surely felt this way when Elisha asked her *what she had in her house*. Just as the words slipped out of her mouth she remembered that she had one last possession—a flask of oil. There has been much conjecture about this flask of oil. As a woman, I think that I know why she kept this oil. I know what I would keep if my husband passed away before me. I would cherish his Bible and his books. The most logical token of her husband's ministry had to be the oil that he used to anoint the sick, a priest, or even a king. It represented the anointing of God.

Today you may feel like you have nothing but I want you to do what the widow did. Find *empty* vessels around your family or city and pour out the anointing that God is placing in you. As you pour into people that are emptier than you, you will discover that the anointing of the Holy Spirit does shatter yokes. Not just their yokes but yours. If you feel empty because of tragedy, trials or a broken heart, ask the Holy Spirit to pour through you. I am convinced that as the anointing is poured into others there will be plenty left over to fill you anew. Go ahead, try. I dare you! It worked for us and it will work for you!

MOMENTS TO REFLECT:

How has Jesus blessed your life in times when you had very little "in your house"?

MOMENTS TO REFRESH:

Realize that as God uses you to touch others, He also blesses your life immensely.

MOMENTS TO REFOCUS:

Direct your thoughts from your needs to the needs of others. Think of people you know who are "emptier" than you.

MOMENTS TO RESPOND:

Plan to help one or more of these people by pouring blessing into their lives from what you have.

Denise Goulet is the executive pastor at the International Church of Las Vegas where her husband, Paul, is the senior pastor. Denise is a commissioned work-

er with International Network of Christian Workers, president of the Las Vegas Resource Center, and a teacher at World Wide School of Ministry. Denise's teaching and preaching connect with women in practical ways, giving them challenging principles to change their lives—physically, mentally and spiritually. Her message of hope to the hopeless and healing to those who are in need of healing has been used to influence women all over the world. She and Paul have three children.

Contact Denise Goulet at: robyng@iclv.com or visit www.iclv.com.

CHAPTER 14

Princess Warrior

Cheryl J. Hansen

The Lord is a warrior.
Exodus 15:3 (NIV)

Women make up more than half of the Lord's fighting force. However, the devil has held us back from achieving our full potential. We are called to be princess warriors who in all boldness wield the sword of the Spirit to advance the kingdom of God.

We are called to manifest. If the devil can manifest an evil spirit then if we are truly possessed by God we should manifest His *Holy Spirit*. A woman of God must be weaned from the mother's milk of self-concern and step into the battle of winning souls and making disciples.

When my husband and I had our daughter, Hannah Jean, my mother suddenly turned into a different woman; she became a grandmother. Suddenly, before anyone would ask, she was impulsively pulling out her purse and proudly presenting the latest portfolio of photos. "Isn't my grandbaby just adorable? What a precious little treasure," she would say to anyone and everyone within reach. She was being the town crier about the newest addition to our family.

We do not need another Sunday School class or correspondence course on evangelism. We just need to fall madly in love with Jesus. Because whatever you love, you will talk about passionately—whether it's your grandbabies, cooking, sewing, computers or exercising. It's time to manifest your faith. It's time to demonstrate your love. It's time to speak about the priceless treasure you have found in Jesus.

Warriors know their enemies. In electronics, a resistor is a device that holds back power. In my extensive ministry with women, I've noticed that some obstacles act as resistors. They inhibit the manifestation of faith. These fall into three categories.

First is *a poor understanding of biblical authority.* Babies don't understand authority. Woman of God, it's time to come under your God-granted authority. A generation of young females sees many of us fighting over the color of the church's carpet, burning up the phone lines with gossip, fighting over whose turn it is to work in the nursery and listening to Oprah Winfrey more than reading the Word. Submit to the authority God has set over you as a sergeant submits to his general. Then you'll see blessing and victory flow from the fountain of your faith.

Second, *false gods* attempt to limit the manifestation of your faith. You might say, "I don't have any false gods." Look a little closer. Perhaps we'll uncover the false gods of comfort, fun, and self-image.

Do you spend more time putting on your makeup and doing your hair than you spend with Jesus? Do you spend more money on eating out or dog food than on missions giving? Are you more concerned about the extra weight you have around your middle than the weight of the lost souls around your neighborhood? These false gods hold us back. We are commanded to cast "down arguments and every high thing that exalts itself against the knowledge of God" (2 Corinthians 10:5, NKJV). These modern day enemies must be utterly destroyed if you are to possess all that the Father has given you.

Third is a *lack of commitment*. Jesus needs you to be tough-skinned yet tenderhearted. You can't be someone who gets her feelings hurt easily, because *this is war!*

There's no time to lick old wounds. The world is dying from the disease called sin and we hold the only cure. It's time to lead! No more should've, could've, would've! Today determine to manifest your faith. "For the eyes of the Lord range throughout the earth to strengthen those whose hearts are fully committed to him" (2 Chronicles 16:9, NIV). He will strengthen you as your commitment is manifest.

It's called service. If you were to join any branch of the military it would also be said that you had joined the service. You *are* in the service, even if you don't realize it. When you gave your heart to Jesus you signed up for military service, with your primary mission being to win souls and make disciples (see Matthew 28:19). Here are 10 important characteristics of the 21st-century princess warrior.

Princess Warriors:

- Learn to deal with inconveniences and discomfort (Philippians 4:12).
- Are not easily distracted (Hebrews 12:2).
- Obey authority and treat those in authority with respect (1 Timothy 2:2).
- Learn discipline and then are promoted to disciple others (Matthew 25:23).
- Are concerned for their fellow soldiers and will leave no one behind (Philippians 2:3).
- Always carry their weapons (2 Corinthians 10:4).
- Are always advancing the kingdom of God (Matthew 11:12).
- Are not perfect, simply committed (Hebrews 11:1).
- Are led into battle through Spirit-filled worship (2 Chronicles 20:21).
- Don't covet comfort, they crave conquest (Romans 8:37).

There's a time for war. King Solomon in all his wisdom reminds us that to everything there is a season—"a time for war" (Ecclesiastes 3:8). Moses led the Children of Israel out of bondage in Egypt. However, it was Joshua who called the Israelites to war in order to go in and possess the land. It's not enough just to "come out" of the captivity of sin. Princess warriors are being called to "go in" and possess all the promises of God for our lives, our families, and our children. My challenge to you is to step up and join the ever-growing ranks of princess warriors. Put on your armor, ladies, and let's *charge!*

Look out, devil. I'm taking back what you've stolen from me and I'm not going to back down, back up, shut up or quit. I'm going into my promised land dressed in the full battle armor of God—as a princess warrior!

MOMENTS TO REFLECT:

Answer this question: Was I trained as a child to be a warrior or a worrier?

MOMENTS TO REFRESH:

Memorize 2 Chronicles 16:9.

MOMENTS TO REFOCUS:

Rank these in order of importance in your life: worship, wealth, warfare, worry, and witness.

MOMENTS TO RESPOND:

Pray out loud: "Father, Exodus 15:3 says that You are a 'Warrior' and I know that I have been made in Your image. Therefore, today, through faith, I choose to see myself as You designed me. I am a princess warrior. I am in the service of my King and will not be defeated! In Jesus name, amen."

Cheryl J. Hansen is associate pastor in charge of Sisterhood, the Women's Network at First Assembly of God in Springfield, Illinois. First Assembly is a cell-based church dedicated to winning souls and making disciples. Cheryl is married to Eric and has one daughter, Hannah Jean. Besides her pastoral duties, Cheryl is also degreed in piano performance and plays for the church's worship team. As well, Cheryl enjoys being a registered nurse, ministering in the hospital to cancer patients. Pastor Hansen loves Jesus, her family and helping other women discover that they, too, can become princess warriors.

Contact Cheryl Hansen at: PastorCheryl@firstaog.org.

CHAPTER 15

Be the Best

Peggy Horn

*And whatever you do, do it heartily, as to the Lord
and not to men.*
Colossians 3:23 (NKJV)

I have always wanted my older brother to be proud of me. As a child, I would do just about anything that he dared me to do and then suffer the consequences, just because I didn't want to disappoint him.

When I married a minister I decided that I would be the best pastor's wife I could be. I had a wonderful mentor in Barbara Horwege, my senior pastor's wife. She could do everything! Before Ken and I were married Barbara would often send him back to the church annex where he lived to change clothes that didn't quite match. The best was that green sports coat and red tie!

I never expected to match her musically, an area in which she was very gifted—she led the choir and played the piano. I did sit at the piano a few times and pray that the Lord would miraculously teach me to play. Imagine a pastor's wife who couldn't play the piano!

I watched Barbara. In our first pastorate I taught Sunday School, led children's church, entertained, did visitation . . . I even played the organ. We sang "Amazing Grace" almost every Sunday since I only knew about three songs. If we didn't sing it, I played it as an offertory.

In our second pastorate I was still trying to do it all. At a get-together we played a game where each person put a little-known fact about themselves in a basket and then, as those were drawn, people guessed whom it was about. I wrote on my slip of paper, "I have had 33 jobs." When it was pulled, one woman said, "I don't know who this is but she's sure a flake!" Quickly, in defense, I responded, "No, I'm a pastor's wife!"

I have come to realize that God hasn't asked me to do it all—just what He asks. Sometimes, that changes. In our last pastorate I realized that I loved being in the background; I loved the kitchen. I decided to be the best in the kitchen I could be. The ladies knew they could usually find me there. And there I was willing to talk with them, share with them, pray with them and laugh with them . . . which we did a lot!

Recognizing our limitations can be hard. We need to realize that all God asks is that we be obedient with the gifts He has given us. He is the potter and like the clay we need His shaping and His molding (see Jeremiah 18). The process is hard and long . . . and it can hurt. We ultimately need to go through the firing process to strengthen us.

I realize that, in our ministry, God has not asked me to do just one thing, but many. He has used me at different times in unique and various ways. He has gifted me at times to accomplish things I never thought possible.

In the days of communism, Ken and I were involved in ministry behind the Iron Curtain. Who would have thought that a pastor's wife who loved the kitchen would be used in such a way? We ministered together and saw tremendous miracles as God guided us in getting materials to Christians who were being persecuted and imprisoned for their faith. We prayed together for their needs, for healing and protection. We were privileged to see God move mightily.

On our last trip behind the Iron Curtain, Ken became seriously ill. We returned home to drastically changed lives. We faced the stark realization that we would be unable to continue our ministry and we possibly would never pastor again. As I cared for Ken and worked a secular job, I thought of our years of ministry and wondered if it was over.

One day, I sat hopelessly on the side of the bed. "God," I said, "I can't take any more!" As soon as those words were out of my mouth I heard a crash in the bathroom and realized that Ken had just collapsed . . . again.

Looking back on that now, it appears that God may have a sense of humor. But at the time I was exhausted and frustrated . . . with where we were and with my faith. I never lost faith in God, but I became very weary. Today I realize how very important were those who supported us. We needed others to pray, because a lot of the time we were just unable to do it ourselves.

We eventually came through that illness and were able to pastor again. In retrospect, God was teaching us some crucial lessons. We feel we became much better pastors, with more understanding and compassion for those in need than before.

Now our lives have changed again. My husband works at the Assemblies of God headquarters in Springfield, Missouri. During his long office hours and frequent travel, I am no longer alongside him. We no longer function as a couple in ministry. All of a sudden I had lost my identity as a pastor's wife, a job I loved and took very seriously.

Once again God asked me just to be obedient and do what He asks. There was a time of rest. Then, a wonderful surprise. I started working with a compassion ministry called Convoy of Hope. When I started going on the outreaches, I once again felt like I had to do it all. I worked alongside the men (all of whom are much younger than I), and I would pound stakes, put up fencing, carry boxes, anything that needed doing. I was going to be the best at what I was doing.

I have been doing this for a few years now and have learned once again that I only need be obedient to God. I don't need to show the guys how much I can do. I now do what's needed but often leave the heavy work to the younger guys. Teen Challenge has been a great blessing in this area—those guys are strong!

Now as I look at where I have been and where God is leading, I see many things I did wrong, and even times I rebelled. But I also see an exciting life that God has led me through, asking only one thing: that I be willing to do what He asks, when He asks, and do it all the best I can.

MOMENTS TO REFLECT:
Have you been doing what God asks or are you doing your own thing hoping it's His will?

MOMENTS TO REFRESH:
Take time to think about the many good things God has brought into your life through the things He has asked you to do.

MOMENTS TO REFOCUS:
What can you do to make the most of your time and energy?

MOMENTS TO RESPOND:
Pray: Lord, what do You want with my life and what can I do to be all You ask?

Peggy Horn is the national outreach coordinator for Convoy of Hope. She participates in Convoy events as a national team member, speaks at churches and trains volunteers. Peggy has had a long-standing involvement in Women's Ministries and Missionettes. She and her husband, Ken, reside in Springfield, Missouri.

Contact Peggy Horn at: phorn@convoyofhope.org.

CHAPTER 16

Finding Purpose in Life: Completing Your "To Do" List

Linda Huddleston

All the days ordained for me were written in your book
before one of them came to be.
Psalm 139:16 (NIV)

When you get up every morning, start the day with a question, "Why has God allowed me to live one more day?" The plan God has for your life is obviously not complete. Jesus knew He had completed all He came to do when He said, "It is finished." He had done all God had intended for Him to do. So, what else is there for you to do here on earth? On your journey what is in God's plan for you to do today? Obviously He's not finished with you yet.

For women, it all starts with Eve. God's purpose for creating woman was to help man. Genesis 2:18 says, "It is not good for the man to be alone. I will make a helper suitable for him." Man's first helper was Eve.

What did God know about women that He knew we would be good for men? In His design of the woman how did she fit into His ultimate plan? God, being God, only works in the realm of perfection. What in our character—our makeup—is there to make men look good, to help them to be all that God has called and designed them to be? What is it about the woman that completes the man?

Women, we are the bomb! You see, as helpers we are still created in God's image. Being a helper is a very powerful and influential position. We must be good at what we do because God does not make junk. Think about a Fortune 500 company; when they look for an assistant for their CEO/president, how qualified are the candidates? Are they slobs, mediocre or very qualified? Their purpose is to make their boss look good, so the company seeks out the very best. Well, do you think that God would give man a helper that would not make him look good? No!

We need to take pride in how we perform our role. It's all about relationships, and it starts with God; we were created to be in fellowship with Him.

We need to embrace all that God wants us to be. Do not covet what you are not. If you are pushing someone up a ladder, every time that person steps up a notch, guess what . . . you do, too. When that person gets to the top, guess who's up there with him? You are!

As women, every human being who comes into this world comes through us. We have the awesome responsibility and privilege of nurturing them. Who they become has a lot to do with us as mothers—as women.

God has an order for everything. Anything with two heads is a freak. Someone has got to have the authority to have the last word in areas where you don't agree. Man submits to God, and the woman submits to man—ouch! It's not for me to say, "Lord, I'll do it if the other person will do it." God is looking for us to say, "Yes, I will obey what You have commanded me to do." In helping someone else fulfill his purpose and dreams, you are fulfilled.

My husband, Samuel Huddleston, was a wounded, broken and insecure man when I first met him. My job was to come alongside and help him to become all that God had called and designed him to be. As his wife I felt my number one responsibility was to be his intercessor. Fasting and praying for his journey and my success in getting him there were top priorities on my list.

When Samuel and I got married, his ambition was to be a gardener like his dad. I told him that was good. I said, "After you get a doctoral degree you can start your gardening business." This was in 1976. He will be graduating from Regent University in Virginia Beach in 2005 with his doctorate.

While fulfilling his purpose we have traveled to Italy, Africa and Israel several times. He's been to Egypt, England, France, Costa Rica, Belize and other places. This he never would have dreamed—neither did I as I was pushing and encouraging him.

You see, there is absolutely nothing wrong with being a gardener. It's a fantastic job. But Samuel was settling for that because he thought that was all he could do. But God had a different plan for his life. I had to encourage him to prepare himself to be the best gardener he could be.

Now he is a gardener. He plants seed—the Word of God—and he reaps a harvest of souls for Christ. As his helper sometimes I had to plant things in his heart. Other times I had to water what someone else had planted. And God has faithfully given the increase.

So, what is your purpose? Jesus' purpose was to bring salvation to a dying world. His posture was that of a servant. He washed feet. He was the One with the towel over His shoulders. He did not focus within, but He looked out to see and went out of His way to serve others—His disciples, the woman at the well, Mary and Martha, and others.

This principle applies in all areas of life, not just marriage. Whom has God called you to serve? Are you doing it as unto the Lord, out of obedience to Him?

No one else on earth can fulfill your purpose—only you. If you don't pursue it someone will miss out, because in this world it all flows together. We need each other. We can't make it without each other.

MOMENTS TO REFLECT:

How have you used each day God has given you? Have you fulfilled your purpose?

MOMENTS TO REFRESH:

"'For I know the plans I have for you,' declares the Lord, 'plans to prosper you and not to harm you, plans to give you hope and a future'" (Jeremiah 29:11).

MOMENTS TO REFOCUS:

As an ambassador for Christ, what is my purpose for this day?

MOMENTS TO RESPOND:

Whom can I serve today, whom can I encourage, motivate, help, give a kind word to? Whom can I let know someone cares by calling, sending a note, giving a smile? God, what is my "to do" list for today?

Linda Huddleston, born in Madera, California, was raised by her grandmother who took her to church where she was taught the Word and accepted Christ as a child. One of her favorite things to do is to get alone in a quiet place and read the Bible for hours.

Linda and her husband, Pastor Samuel M. Huddleston, founded Lighthouse Covenant Fellowship Assembly of God, in Benicia, California, in 1993. Linda is a graduate of Bethany College, Santa Cruz, California. A speaker in her own right, Linda has spoken for various women's conferences and groups including Women's Aglow International. Currently she is the Women's Ministries leader and music minister in her home church. The Huddlestons have been married 27 years. They have three children and seven grandchildren who all serve the Lord.

Contact Linda Huddleston at: mamahudd@mail.iglide.net.

CHAPTER 17

Dealing with Death

Doris P. Johnson

In my distress *and* anguish, *your*
commandments comfort me.
Psalm 119:143 (TLB)
I weep with grief; my heart is heavy with sorrow;
encourage and cheer me with your words.
Psalm 119:28

My childhood world caved in on a spring afternoon of
my 11th year. Why was Dad's car in the driveway so early?
And the pastor's? My pastor took my hand and tearfully
informed me that my mother had just gone to be with
Jesus. I began sobbing as he read Psalm 23, familiar verses I had memorized years before. If God really loved me,
why would He take away the person who loved me most?
On Saturday nights Mother and I rode the streetcar across

Detroit to prayer meeting at our downtown church and she often treated me to a chocolate candy bar afterwards.

In the passing months I missed Mother terribly, as well as my seven younger siblings who were farmed out to Christian homes. I often cried myself to sleep, only to awaken hearing my father pleading with God to send a mother for his children so we could once again serve Him all together. Though earthly poor, Dad was rich in faith and had taught us to trust in the daily Scriptures we memorized at family altar.

Someone has said that the Bible is the lifeline God throws us to stay connected while awaiting rescue. Because of my father's stubborn faith and importunate pleadings, God rescued us through a wonderful lady named Juanita who had just lost her husband and only child in a boating accident. Juanita adopted all eight of us children and our father as well! She worked two full-time jobs so I could finish high school and college, preparing for ministry. Her weekly letters during the next 30 years kept us connected while an ocean apart.

Three years into overseas ministry, my dear father-in-law passed away suddenly, leaving sorrowing congregations, a widowed mother with three children, and heavy ministry burdens. We were overwhelmed with grief. But God's Word proved to be the daily balm of Gilead, soothing our wounded spirits.

Our next great loss was two younger brothers, my husband Bernhard's and mine. His brother, Felipe, was only 23, newly ordained, a successful youth evangelist with a powerful preaching and singing ministry. Flying home to

San Jose from Seattle, fighting tears and questions, I heard a gentle whisper: "I took him to spare him 'from the evil *to come*'" (Isaiah 57:1, KJV). My backslidden brother died at 37, leaving a grieving widow with five small children. One year later the Holy Spirit comforted us through a distant stranger's word of knowledge that he had indeed repented on his deathbed, thus honoring our family's years of intercession.

In the next decade we lost my precious mother-in-law, a veteran missionary, as well as my own parents after extended suffering. Two years of home care drained my sisters and me physically, emotionally, and spiritually. But for the daily intercession of family and prayer partners, we never could have survived that fiery trial including a vicious lawsuit. I clung daily to Psalm 71:16: "I will go in the strength of the Lord God." As I went, worked, served, traveled, and ministered, God supplied the needed strength.

Grief invaded our lives again in 1994 when our fourth grandchild arrived for only two hours before returning to heaven. As I wept on the phone with my faithful prayer partner, Ramona Crabtree, the Spirit spoke through her, "Do not weep for this child whom I have taken unto Myself." The words of Ezekiel 24:16 consoled our broken hearts once more.

But the darkest hour was just 11 months later, losing my beloved soul mate and ministry partner of 43 years after a sudden heart attack. The indescribable agony of sudden loss of marriage and ministry was like surgery without anesthesia, sucking the very life out of body, soul, and spirit. Numbing depression paralyzed normal functions as I dragged myself through painful days and sleepless nights. I begged God to take me home, for life seemed worthless without the joy of seeing multitudes saved, healed, and delivered. Healing came unexpectedly one late summer afternoon after a long workday. My living room suddenly filled with an overwhelming heavenly fragrance and that familiar gentle whisper, "Whose crusades were they?"

"Well, Lord, they were Yours."

"Then why don't you give them back to Me?"

In that moment of surrender, my fountain of tears dried up as waves of peace took its place. Thus began the first step of a long journey to wholeness and restoration. Are you facing overwhelming loss? Seize the Word of God as your lifeline. Hang on tightly until rescue comes.

REMEMBER . . . God loves you as much as He loved your spouse or loved one. Just because He gave you less responsibility doesn't mean He loves you less. You are the apple of His eye. Rejoice and be comforted!

MOMENTS TO REFLECT:
Humbly accept the prayers of loved ones and fellow believers.

MOMENTS TO REFRESH:
Take time to bathe daily in the cleansing, nourishing Word of God. Accept each day's healing with gratitude.

MOMENTS TO REFOCUS:

Resist the lies and oppression of your adversary.

MOMENTS TO RESPOND:

Step out in faith, no matter how weak you feel, physically and spiritually.

Doris P. Johnson served in full-gospel ministry for 51 years, the last 46 being in foreign missions. For 30 years she and her late husband, Dr. Bernhard Johnson Jr., led evangelism crusades on six continents with a harvest of 1.8 million decisions for Christ.

She was educated at the Detroit Institute of Arts, Central Bible College, San Jose State University, and Bethany College, Santa Cruz, California.

She travels extensively in the U.S.A. and Brazil speaking for missions conventions, women's conferences, and prayer retreats. She contributes to several publications, and is involved in the Brazil Extension School of Theology, Brazil Advanced School of Theology, Rio Pentecostal Bible Institute, Children of Brazil Outreach, and HealthCare Ministries clinics.

Doris has three children: Beth Mapes, Terry Johnson (president of Bernhard Johnson Ministries, Brazil), and David Johnson. She also has five grandchildren and two great-grandchildren.

Contact Doris Johnson at: bjministries@sbcglobal.net.

CHAPTER 18

Drawing Near to God

Maria Khaleel

Draw near to God and He will draw near to you.
James 4:8 (NASV)

Could it be that how close we are to God depends wholly upon us? Could anyone be privileged to know God as Moses knew Him, for "the Lord used to speak to Moses face to face, just as a man speaks to his friend" (Exodus 33:11)? Is this attainable to anyone who desires it? J. Oswald Sanders said, "We are at this moment, as close to God as we really choose to be." [1]

God is revealed as One who speaks, who comes down in the stream of human experience and makes himself known. From the beginning, He came down and shared intimate fellowship with Adam and Eve. What severed that relationship came not from God but man. Clearly, man's closeness to God is not changed by what happens on God's side, but what happens on man's side.

How close to God do you desire to be? There are times when our soul truly longs for a closer relationship with God, but when it comes down to it, many times we are not prepared to pay the price. So we simply settle for a less demanding, though woefully less satisfying, level of Christian living, and our longing for God languishes as wishful thinking.

Matt Redman, a noted worship leader, said, "Worship is about getting personal with God, drawing close to God." Do you truly know God? Who is God to you? Is He but an impersonal force, or is He your Father, whom you know, and with whom you enjoy a personal and intimate relationship?

Worship means to draw near to God. In the sacrificial system of the Old Testament, the Lord provided a divine pattern for worship. Sacrifice was synonymous with worship. One of the important Hebrew words used for these offerings is *karav*. The root meaning is "to come near." Sin is what had separated man from the intimate fellowship God had intended for us to share. Through the sacrifice, the offense of sin could be removed, and the worshiper might once again draw near to God. Jesus Christ has become the ultimate sacrifice for our sin, and the Scripture now declares, "Let us draw near with a sincere heart in full assurance of faith" (Hebrews 10:22). Through the sacrifice of His Son, God has already done everything on His part to make a close and intimate relationship with us possible. Now it is up to us to draw near.

Worship is drawing near to God. It is the key to intimacy with God. Worship is the expression of our desire to know God. In Exodus 33:18, Moses expressed the compelling desire of his life when he said, "I pray Thee, show me Thy glory!" God had promised to send an angel to go with Israel into the Promised Land, but that was not enough for Moses. He pleaded in prayer, "If Thy presence does not go *with us*, do not lead us up from here" (Exodus 33:15), and when God promised His presence, Moses still desired more. He wanted to see God's glory. The ever-deepening desire of his heart was to know God more fully. What is the desire of your heart?

In the New Testament, the disciples overheard Jesus praying and cried out, "Lord, teach us to pray" (Luke 11:1). As Jews, they had probably followed the Jewish practice of praying three times a day, but when they heard Jesus pray there was something different about His prayers. As the disciples overheard their Master praying, they were captivated by the depth of intimacy they sensed He had with the Father. The moment He said "Father" it was as though He had stepped into the very throne room of heaven. As He breathed that opening address, I believe they sensed the presence of God. This was no mere ritual, no empty recitation of words, but this was intimate communion with God. They wanted what Jesus had. The desire to know God was kindled within their own hearts and they asked, "Lord, teach us to pray." Jesus was only too pleased to respond, because this is the very end to which He had been leading them, an ever-deepening knowledge and relationship with the Father. The prayer He taught them began with worship, and is halfway through before ever mentioning anything about requests or petitions. For Jesus, the key to intimacy with God was worship.

Worship is an action. It is something we do that expresses our desire for God. It has been said that "there's a close relationship between our passion and our ability to worship." Desire is what God uses to bring us to himself. David implied this when he wrote, "Delight yourself also in the Lord, and He shall give you the desires of your heart" (Psalm 37:4).[2] When we consider what God has offered to us for seeking a deepening relationship with Him, "It would seem," in the words of C.S. Lewis, "that our Lord finds our desires not too strong, but too weak. We are half-hearted creatures . . . far too easily pleased."[3]

MOMENTS TO REFLECT:

The ultimate longing of the soul is voiced in the words "Whom have I in heaven *but Thee*? And besides Thee, I desire nothing on earth" (Psalm 73:25). Is this the desire of your soul?

MOMENTS TO REFRESH:

Think of how much God loves you and desires to have a relationship with you, that He was willing to pay the ultimate price in the sacrifice of His Son.

MOMENTS TO REFOCUS:

Spend some time in worship today. May we be so captivated by His presence, may we take delight in His fellowship, and may we have an ever-increasing desire to know Him more.

MOMENTS TO RESPOND:

In prayer, cry out for an ever-deepening relationship with God. "Lord, teach us by Your Spirit how to pray, how to enter into deep and intimate communion with You."

Rev. Maria Khaleel is senior pastor of New Life Assembly of God, a church she pioneered in 1992, in Pembroke Pines, Florida. It is a multicultural congregation with more than 700 in attendance, 80 percent of whom are first-time converts.

A 1986 summa cum laude graduate of Southeastern College, Maria received the "Young Alumnus of the Year Award" in 1994, given to those who within 10 years of graduation have made an outstanding impact in ministry. She completed her M.A. through Assemblies of God Theological Seminary in 2002, and was given the "Outstanding Achievement Student of the Year Award."

She was ordained in 1988, and in 1998 became the first woman to be elected as presbyter in the Peninsular Florida District. She also serves on the National Evangelism Commission, and on the National Women in Ministry Task Force. She preaches nationally and internationally.

Contact Maria Khaleel at: NLPastor@aol.com.

CHAPTER 19

Slow Me Down, Lord

Gloria Lundstrom

Be still, and know that I am *God.*
Psalm 46:10 (KJV)

It was another one of my *normal* days filled with an urgent "to do" list . . . sorting through mail, fulfilling article deadlines, meeting people, and running endless errands. I was already one lap behind in my race. I ran through the hotel lobby in Helena, Montana, lunging toward the front entrance only to be suddenly stopped short by the automatic doors. I had beaten the electric eye that signaled it to open, and there I stood impatiently waiting. I was already three minutes late and I could see my ride waiting on the other side of the glass. I managed a somewhat relaxed smile and waved assuring them that I was on my way. I then grumbled, "Come on, doors, open . . . hurry, hurry!"

As I stood there exasperated, God spoke to my heart, *Gloria, stop! Listen to Me. You're going too fast. Slow down and catch your breath.* Ouch! That hurt! Did God have to be that direct?

I was instantly reminded of what my dad told me a few months earlier. My husband and I were passing through the Phoenix, Arizona, area on a five-month evangelistic tour while my parents were wintering in Apache Junction. I called ahead and we arranged to meet them at the Village Inn restaurant for lunch. When we arrived, they were waiting for us. Larry and I went in, greeted them, sat down and ordered. Knowing we were on a tight schedule, I said, "I'm going to make a quick run to drop film off at the one-hour photo place, mail some letters, and pick up some milk and fruit. I will be right back."

My dad growled, "Sit down, Gloria. Do you always have to be doing 10 things at one time? Now *sit* down and *relax*!" Deflated, I sank into the padded booth.

"Yes, Dad," I apologized, "you're right." I needed that scolding to alert me about my hectic schedule because sometimes I get in such a rush and then lose sight of my destination.

I read a true story once of a famous scholar in Dublin who was a traveling lecturer. Having finished a series of lectures, and knowing he had a tight schedule to reach the next destination, he quickly readied his things for the next day. In the morning, he departed in one of Dublin's famous horse-drawn taxis. Assuming that his business manager had told the driver where to take him, he instructed the driver, "Hurry! I'm almost late! Drive fast!" The horses lurched forward and galloped across the streets of Dublin at a vigorous pace; the scholar sat back and closed his eyes to rest. A while later, he glanced out the window noticing they were going west . . . away from the sun, not toward it. Leaning forward, the scholar shouted to the driver, "Do you know where you are going?"

Without looking back, the driver yelled an unforgettable line: "No, your honor, but I'm driving very fast!"

Did that story ever hit home! Many times that describes me. Does it portray you as well? In the world today, many of us are rushing at great speeds to unknown destinations. That story reminds me to taxi toward the "Son" (Jesus Christ)—not away from Him. God wants us to slow down, not break down. I think I finally have it figured out after living on the road 11 months out of the year for nearly 40 years . . . life is not going to slow down, for me or anyone else. I've realized that I, and only I, with God's help, can change my "out of control" life when I feel like a fast flying Frisbee. It is in those moments God again reminds me of His advice in Psalm 46:10, "Be still, and know that I am God," and I recognize that I need to stop and reorganize my priorities.

To spend time with God gives me peace. To spend time in prayer and His Word gives me power. To spend time with Him directs me to what my real priorities are and should be.

Maybe now as you have read this devotional, God is prompting you to stop, slow down, listen, draw close and rest in Him. Do it now. You won't regret it.

MOMENTS TO REFLECT:
God help me reflect on how much You love me and want me to live a peace-filled life.

MOMENTS TO REFRESH:
Let me be refreshed by spending time in Your presence. Help me not to get caught up in the "rush" of the day but rather in the power of Your presence.

MOMENTS TO REFOCUS:
Help me, Father, to refocus on Your destination . . . to run to the Son of God for spiritual refreshment and nourishment.

MOMENTS TO RESPOND:
May I respond immediately to Your still, small voice when You whisper, "Be still. Take time to know Me."

Gloria Lundstrom is the wife of evangelist Larry Lundstrom from Sisseton, South Dakota. Lundstrom Evangelistic Ministries is currently reaching people in the U.S.A. and Canada. She is the mother of two daughters, LaShawn and LaDawn, and one son, Donovan. She takes great delight in being the grandmother to Danté and Myanna. Gloria, Larry, and family traveled extensively as a central part of Lowell Lundstrom Ministries for more than 22 years. For the past 20 years, Larry and Gloria have been conducting "Heart to Heart" rallies from coast to coast helping strengthen families in crisis.

During her 38 years of ministry, Gloria has spoken at numerous district, regional and state women's retreats, conventions, churches and banquets. At these various functions, Gloria challenges women to honestly look at the struggles and joys of everyday life and find hope amidst life's chaos. She wants all women to "come to be heartened in truth that our own experiences of suffering and love, of breakdown and breakthrough, are sacred."

Gloria has also written Free at Last, *a book that shares her testimony of how God set her free. Her speaking tapes have become a significant tool of growth and encouragement.*

Contact Gloria Lundstrom (or learn more about her ministry) at: www.larrylundstromministries.org.

CHAPTER 20

Faith in Everyday Life

Audrey Manning

I have been crucified with Christ and I no longer live,
but Christ lives in me. The life I live in the body,
I live by faith in the Son of God, who loved me
and gave himself for me.
Galatians 2:20 (NIV)

Faith is needed for Christians to live upon this earth. It is as needed for our spiritual well-being as food and water are needed for our physical existence. We live by faith in Jesus Christ.

Born into a Christian family, I was taught to have faith in God at an early age. "We live by faith" was a statement frequently heard in our home. My parents declared that during the Great Depression we never went hungry. God supplied our needs in unusual ways.

One night my father went outside because the dog was barking. He shined the flashlight on a tree and saw what he thought to be a hawk. He took his .22 rifle and shot it. When the bird tumbled out of the tree, he found, instead, a big wild turkey. My parents had been asking God for meat, and He supplied it.

This faith in everyday life was needed—and manifested—during our family's missionary work in Chile. During a three-year period of scarcity of provisions in the nation, we had money but there was little food to buy. We prayed daily, asking God to supply our needs. He did . . . by supplying us with meat, chicken, flour, butter, coffee, and all sorts of things in wonderful ways. We never went hungry. Our God took care of us!

Once, arsenic contaminated our city's drinking water and hundreds of people died. I became very ill and couldn't retain food or water. The doctor could do nothing. But Jesus could, and with faith in Him I was wonderfully healed.

On another occasion, my husband was in the States attending his father's funeral. I stood looking down at the rubbish that the firemen had thrown into our yard from the house. Emotionally I was hurting. A wave of depression swept over me. This was the second house fire in our married life. When the firemen had left, I walked through the shell of the house to the backyard. My eyes focused on a dead sparrow on the ground. Jesus spoke to me in my spirit: *You are more valuable than this sparrow, yet I saw it fall.* What love the Father has for us!

As I returned to the front yard, standing there, I said, "Oh, Jesus, I cannot go on sorting through the burnt things, losing everything again. I'll pack a small suitcase and return to the States and there we can start over." All at once I noticed something yellow in the trash, so I took my foot and moved the ashes aside. There with its head held high was a yellow pansy. Jesus whispered softly, *This is another one of My creations. It has been trampled on by the firemen and weighted down by all this rubbish, and yet it has not been destroyed, nor overcome, nor defeated. It has lifted its head again.*

I said, "Oh, Jesus, thank You for reminding me that faith in You will see me through." Yes, faith in God every day, during good and bad times will sustain us.

As I write this, I am looking at our backyard where there is a beautiful new swing set for our 5-year-old granddaughter who lives with us. I had little money and had asked God to supply a swing set with the money I had. Faith in Him can do even that. My husband, Bruce, went to a store to get something and there in the window was a sign. "Swing sets, 70 percent off, today only," it said. It was the amount I had.

Living by faith every day changes the impossible to the possible as we put our faith in a God who is bigger than our problems.

MOMENTS TO REFLECT:

Love and faith walk hand in hand. When we can comprehend how much God loves us, it is easier to reach out to Him by simple faith and receive the answer to the petition we bring before Him.

MOMENTS TO REFRESH:

Ponder how much God loves you and wants to give good gifts to His children. Think about the things He has done for you and thank Him for them.

MOMENTS TO REFOCUS:

Daily read the Word and pray. The Bible says, "Consequently, faith comes from hearing the message, and the message is heard through the word of Christ" (Romans 10:17, NIV).

MOMENTS TO RESPOND:

What is the need in your life? Health, finances, healing in the family, peace, or breaking a bad habit? Reach out in faith to your God now. By faith you will receive your answer. Repeat daily, "The life I live in the body, I live by faith in the Son of God." Yes, practice your faith every day!

Audrey Manning is an ordained minister with the Assemblies of God. She and husband Bruce served as missionaries for 40 years in Chile. Audrey worked with the women of Chile, serving as both district and national director of Women's Ministries for most of that time. She also served for more than 10 years as district and national Sunday School director.

Audrey has also served as assistant pastor of 10 churches in the U.S.A. and Chile. She is bilingual, preaching and teaching in Spanish and English. She has planned and spoken at ministers' wives retreats, serving as keynote speaker for women's groups in Central and South America and several districts in the United States.

Contact Audrey Manning at: amanning2@msn.com.

Seasons of a Woman's Life

Jean Meppelink

*As long as the earth endures, seedtime and harvest, cold
and heat, summer and winter, day and
night will never cease.*
Genesis 8:22 (NIV)

For many years, through the 19-foot window of my living room, I watched as the early spring skunk cabbage grew green in the wooded area behind the house.

Regardless of what was going on inside the house, the seasons came and went. Our son grew up and left home, a niece came to live with us, a new baby girl joined the family, and sickness and health took turns visiting. Sometimes there was laughter, other times tears, but the seasons kept their routine as God promised Noah they would.

God said there would be lights in the expanse of the sky to mark seasons and days and years (Genesis 1:14). He set great timing devices in the heavens, the sun and the moon, to give direction to all His creatures for hibernation, migration, planting and harvest. So certain are the seasons that no scientist or meteorologist questions their existence or disputes their schedule.

Seasons speak of change.

Spring brings new life. Trees bud. Flowers grow. The chirping of baby birds and the smell of freshly washed earth remind us of the season.

Summer warms us with its sunshine, longer days and a break from the routine of school or work.

Autumn offers pleasant, cool evenings. Picnics and family cookouts are replaced with football games and a final harvest. The days become shorter, the nights longer.

As winter approaches, birds begin their flight to warmer climates and people prepare home and family for the cooler days ahead.

One thing that is certain in this life: change will come! Whether it is world leaders, weather patterns, lifestyles, economics, ecology, or the family structure—all will be different in just a few years.

Each season has its own particular characteristics and challenges. Age is a relative term. "Young" can mean 3 years old or 25, maybe even 40, depending on a person's perspective. To Grandma, 8 years old is a "baby," but to the mother of four children under 8, great expectations are put on the 8-year-old. Birthdays become touchstones that impress us with the rush of time.

The *springtime* of childhood is full of hope, and youthful energy brings periods of great fun and joy. It has more physical growth and change than any other time. Pictures quickly get outdated. Ideals, opinions, trust, and self-esteem are formed and become a part of the personality. Little thought is given to future seasons. Living is for now, and self is most important.

The *summertime* of life is a time of momentous decisions . . . the choosing of a profession, of a mate, and of a lifestyle. There is a settling in, a maturity, an instinct that says, "It is time to be established." It is the busiest season of life. We discover we have limitations, that we cannot have it all. Our choices at this point determine the course of our future. Too soon summer is over and we are surprised that changes continue. Some high expectations have had to be laid aside. A feeling of "Is this all there is?" may creep in and thoughts are projected to the years ahead. Somehow time has gone more quickly than expected.

Autumn is a wonderful season of life. It is harvesttime. We eat the fruit of labor past. There is time to think, re-evaluate, even alter our course. We begin to realize how little time we have left and become more focused on reaching the goals that are really important. We have freedom to reverse some earlier decisions—go back to school, work part-time at something we enjoy, develop talents that have been neglected. To the one who is willing to change, this can be a blessed time for growing.

The seasons of life cannot be avoided. We may long for summer again, for the security of childhood or the strength of youth, but we cannot go back. Relentlessly, time goes on and each season gives way to the next. Surprisingly, we feel some of the same emotions and face some of the same demands we did in earlier seasons. But the greatest challenge still lies ahead.

Winter can be cold, blustery, and lonely, or it can be cozy, warm, and comfortable, depending on who is with you, where you are, and what preparations you have made. To make the transition from an active adult life to a slower pace is probably life's most challenging change of seasons. Some who handled the most difficult of life's decisions refuse to make this one. They try to cling to youth.

Scripture sees old age as the desirable fruition of a good life . . . a satisfying reward. The Lord considers old age as deserving dignity and respect (Leviticus 19:32). The woman of Proverbs 31 has no fear of old age. She has prepared well and is secure.

Walking with the Lord throughout life is the best way to prepare for winter. He helps us put down deep roots of the spirit that withstand the sun of summer, the waning strength of autumn, and the doubts and winds of winter. Beautiful branches will break. Leaves, however lovely, will fall. Neither will fortify us in the storm. It takes deep, stubborn roots to keep the tree standing when the winds of winter blow.

Roots are not for show. Most are unseen. Roots of thankfulness, love, and faith take time to grow strong. They need nurturing throughout summer and into autumn. God provides the climate for good root growing. He knows just how much sunshine, rain, and wind are needed in each life (Colossians 2:7, NIV).

We may never feel completely ready for the next season, but as surely as winter follows autumn, the seasons of life will continue. After 70 years of life and 50 years of marriage, I can still look out the window, a different one now, and watch the seasons as they pass. The seasons God put in place have not changed. As long as the earth endures, they will continue. So get ready! Winter is coming!

MOMENTS TO REFLECT:

Ask: Where am I in the seasons of life? What kind of roots am I nurturing that will help me grow strong for the next season?

MOMENTS TO REFRESH:

King David realized his soul was refreshed when he reviewed all the blessings God had sent his way. He reminded himself that "all the ways of the Lord are loving and faithful" (Psalm 25:10). God is the only One who never changes. His promises are secure. His love endures through every season of life.

MOMENTS TO REFOCUS:

Daily living may distract individuals from their true purpose, but God's Word is like a cold drink of water on a hot summer day or a hot cup of coffee during a winter storm. Allow it to renew your spirit and help you refocus on what God desires for your season of life.

MOMENTS TO RESPOND:

It is not difficult to begin a race. Finishing is the challenge! Paul must have felt this when he said, "If only I may finish the race and complete the task the Lord Jesus has given me" (Acts 20:24). Determine today that you are going to stay true to God through every season of life. God's promises are to those who stand firm, endure, and finish!

Jean Meppelink's personal call to ministry came when as a young teenager she taught Sunday School in her home church. As a pastor's wife for more than 35 years, Jean and her husband, Harvey, pioneered three Assemblies of God churches. Her ministry included the establishing and directing of a nursery school and the organization of a community-wide Bible study for women.

Jean has been active in numerous speaking/teaching seminars. She has self-published seven books, including Peace in the Parsonage, *and several Bible studies for women.*

Family is very important to the Meppelinks and they have been blessed with three children and nine grandchildren. All of them are serving the Lord in their local congregations.

Contact Jean Meppelink (or for information on Growing Life Ministries) at: mepp@worldnet.att.net.

CHAPTER 22

If You Love . . .
You Are a
Success

Angela Ruth Munizzi

And now I will show you the most excellent way.
1 Corinthians 12:31 (NIV)

I have always felt like a failure when I read the great chapter on love—1 Corinthians 13. That is probably part of the reason I rushed through it that one morning in my devotions. How imperfect my love is compared to the description of the love in this chapter!

But, what a surprise when I sensed that the Holy Spirit was actually trying to bring encouragement to me—not guilt and a sense of failure! *Angela, you are missing the point. If you love, you are a success.*

My attention was drawn to 1 Corinthians 12:31, which is actually a precursor to chapter 13. First Corinthians 12 and 14 both teach that we should desire the *gifts* of the Spirit and use them to edify the church. But the apostle Paul ends chapter 12 and introduces chapter 13 by making this emphatic point: "And now I will show you the most excellent way"—love!

Paul wanted us to put things in perspective. The gifts are of great importance, but love is the essential foundation. We can't build anything significant without it. So, if we accept His perfect love for us, respond by loving Him first, and then risk by loving the others He has placed in our lives, we are pleasing to Him and we are successful.

Love is the fruit of a life yielded to the lordship of Christ and the leading of the Holy Spirit. The gifts, great knowledge and even sacrificial activities are all meaningless without love. If we don't have love, the gifts can actually be dangerous. When a talented, charismatic leader uses his or her charm and appeal to build a personal kingdom, the results can be disastrous. Personal kingdoms built without love portray the wrong standard of success.

We tend to measure success by comparing ourselves to the gifted, beautiful, powerful, knowledgeable or wealthy around us. Isn't this what Hollywood and the advertising industry are trying to get us to buy into? They spend millions to create icons for us to emulate and products that we can't live without, if we want to be "somebody." This mind-set has even infiltrated our churches. It is easy to feel inadequate if we don't have one of the more visible spiritual gifts that Sister So-and-so has.

I have fallen prey to this kind of comparison myself. Though I have been privileged to share God's Word and the insight He has given me with many audiences, one of the strongest gifts He has blessed me with is the gift of administration. God has opened doors for me to use this gift in some amazing world-changing ministries. I don't have a degree in business or management, but time and again the Holy Spirit has guided me in the fulfillment of challenging assignments.

As the Lord expanded my sphere of influence in management, He helped me encourage my team members to believe in and cultivate the gifts He had placed in them. I saw some beautiful metamorphoses.

But when I saw women I respected speaking to hundreds and thousands of women, I found myself fighting depression and insecurity. I would think, *That is really what I want to do—share the Word—not administrate*! Could it be that standing in front of a crowd made me feel more significant than being a team member and aiding someone else's ministry?

Our gifts and whether or not they are acknowledged don't make for success—that comes from loving and obeying God with all our hearts and loving others. The Bible says that this is the most excellent way. Although one day the gifts will cease, the fruit of His love can be taken with us into eternity.

My own dear mom was a precious woman of God, a godly pastor's wife and a gifted Bible teacher. Even though Mom was a licensed minister, she was a bit uncomfortable being in front of big audiences and preaching from a pulpit. Yet, ladies came from all over Long Island to attend her weekday Bible classes.

Women who were troubled and hurting called her. Some had psychological disorders and had undergone radical treatments. Their glazed eyes and trembling voices made their chances for recovery and productive lives seem slim. But Mom would speak the Word of God over them, pray with them and show them His love. Some came to our home to iron or help in some small way, because just being around Mom brought hope. She found time to call them friends.

Many went on to live fruitful, healthy Christian lives, changed by the power of God and the love of one of His servants, Grace Morriello.

Some of you reading this may be fighting feelings of failure. Maybe you're a mom, perhaps single, who loves her children and has brought them up in the ways of the Lord. Yet, they are not walking with Him. You wonder if things would have been different if you had made fewer mistakes or if you could have provided more material possessions.

Or, maybe you are a Sunday School teacher. You have taught year after year and poured yourself out for those kids, yet you don't see much fruit.

Perhaps you are a professional woman in a demanding career. You are diligent, honest and attentive to little details that nobody sees. You reach out to your co-workers, sharing Christ with them, praying with them. But you feel discouraged and weary, and long to do something more "spiritual."

You might be saying, "I could never sing or speak like so-and-so." But you spend time alone with God and journal, or you write to encourage a friend, or bake a cake to make someone feel welcome. You might feel like what you are doing really doesn't matter because nobody sees it.

Be encouraged. Stop comparing yourself to others. When you read the Bible's chapters on the gifts and love, don't feel inadequate or guilty. Instead, know that if you have accepted God's unconditional love for yourself, and if you make a choice to love Him and those He has placed in your life, you have chosen the *most excellent* way. You are a success!

MOMENTS TO REFLECT:

Take some time to meditate and pray. Have you been working harder and harder to achieve success? Have you been fighting feelings of failure and insignificance? Have you coveted others' gifts? If so, why?

MOMENTS TO REFRESH:

Ask God to breathe new life into you. Receive His unconditional love. As you reach out with His love to others, be encouraged that your life is having an impact. Give the Lord your gifts, no matter how small you think they may be. Place them on a foundation of love, and let the Lord anoint you and touch others through you.

MOMENTS TO REFOCUS:

Remember that your love for the Lord and those He has placed around you is important and significant. Only eternity will reveal the fruit. Take your eyes off what you don't have, and focus on what God has given you to love and serve others. In what ways can you love those whom the Lord has placed in your sphere of influence?

MOMENTS TO RESPOND:

Has "how" you serve overshadowed "whom" and "why" you serve? Consecrate your life to the Lord and seek Him, not His gifts. Let God deposit His love within your heart, so that in whatever you do, you will bring glory to Him and your love will be genuine, sincere and reflect Him. Be encouraged and know that when you love Him and those He has placed in your life, you have chosen the *most excellent way. You are a success.*

Angela Ruth Munizzi is a minister with the Assemblies of God. She has been involved in a variety of ministries, including office manager for Dr. Bill Bright of Campus Crusade for Christ, partner development specialist with Benny Hinn Ministries, development coordinator for Chi Alpha Campus Ministries, middle school Bible teacher, and co-host of a Christian radio and TV program in the New York metropolitan area. Angela helped to found a forum that mobilized the citizenry of Central Florida to interface and pray with local and state government officials.

Her public speaking encourages people to move from the ordinary to the supernatural. She is the daughter of parents who were both ministers. Her husband, David Munizzi, is the New York District director of Chi Alpha Campus Ministries, and together they have pioneered two college ministries in the Central Florida area.

Angela attended Zion Bible Institute in East Providence, Rhode Island, and later earned a degree in music from the State University of New York, Empire State College.

Married for 32 years, Angela and David have two daughters.

Contact Angela Munizzi at: TwoLiv4Him@aol.com.

CHAPTER 23

Desperate for God

Judy Myrick

When she heard about Jesus, she came up behind him in the crowd and touched his cloak, because she thought, "If I just touch his clothes, I will be healed."
Mark 5:27,28 (NIV)
Read Mark 5:24-34

As a hospital chaplain I've ministered to many people at the point of their desperation. I've often observed that desperation brings about a birthing of faith. It is during their point of desperation that many people will begin to grope uncertainly for God.

Many have been beaten by life so badly that they think there is no hope. Others have had a lukewarm relationship with the Lord and are now fearful that, with death looming, that wasn't enough. Still others have deep emotional wounds from being abused; those who were abusers don't think Jesus can forgive them. There are those who can't forgive themselves for the choices they've made. Many have a hard time accepting the love of a God who would send His only Son to die for them so that they might be forgiven and saved.

Mark 5 tells of a woman who was very much in need due to a 12-year issue of blood. She was an outcast by Jewish law. Anything that she touched or sat on was considered unclean; if she was married, she couldn't have relations with her husband and she couldn't go to "church" (synagogue). Doctors' bills had left her financially destitute. She was very weak and alone.

I've sensed that many of my patients feel alone in their desperation. I am able to relate to them because I have faced some desperate situations myself—and God has blessed me by helping me through.

I was a young mother with two children when I was diagnosed with a brain tumor. I felt frightened and alone. Those emotions were repeated when seven doctors told me that my youngest child would not live long enough for me to see her again. The passage in Mark became reality for me. I felt as if I was "groping" for God and His will in these difficult circumstances. Sometimes I wasn't even sure if I knew how to pray. Christians weren't always helpful. Some accused me of a lack of faith. God would heal me without surgery if I had enough faith, they said. The truth is, sometimes God's best will is to give us our new home in eternity. God helped me to accept His will, whatever it might be, for myself and my child. Then He healed us both.

I have found the following steps helpful to those who are struggling to touch God in the midst of desperate situations. Each subject should be meditated upon one at a time.

Grasp the reality of who Jesus is. Is God's Word true? Did Jesus die for me? Is Jesus the same yesterday, today, and forever? Did Jesus really heal and meet people's needs and does He still heal and meet needs today? Has all power been given to Jesus?

Receive His promises. How might I "touch the hem of His garment"?

I once had a patient who was given a diagnosis of imminent death due to cancer. She had been a strong Christian all of her life; however, her countenance appeared very concerned. I thought that she was frightened of dying. Not so! She said, "I'm afraid to take pain medication; it might cause me to say or do something unpleasing to the Lord. I don't want to embarrass my Jesus." We talked about Jesus never being too early or too late meeting our needs. After we prayed, she felt assured that Jesus would indeed be present as needed through this valley and would protect her from that concern. Prayer brought peace to her at that difficult time in her life. She had received Jesus' promise: "I will never leave you nor forsake you."

Obey the still small voice of the Holy Spirit. I believe that the woman in Mark heard the Holy Spirit say, *Go, child, go. Touch this Jesus; you will be made whole.* This woman received enough faith in her desperation to press through a crowd of people who considered her an outcast.

Press through the trial you are going through. The woman in Mark took action in response to the voice of the Holy Spirit and pressed through the crowds until she "touched Jesus." When we touch Jesus, we invite His power to flow into our lives and meet our needs in our weakness.

Invite Jesus to extend His power in your weakness (2 Corinthians 12:9). I had to be honest with Jesus as I went through the personal trials I mentioned above. There were times that I said to the Lord, "I don't know how to pray. I know Your Word says that You will not give me more than I can bear, but it seems I'm mighty close to more than I can bear. Lord, I'm choosing to believe Your Word." Jesus never once condemned me for being honest with Him. He patiently met my needs and allayed my fears with His power. Tell Him your deepest thoughts. Talk to the Lord as if He were sitting next to you. He is.

Now is the time. Jesus wants to touch you. He will not force himself on you. Realize that He is awaiting your invitation for His will to be done in your life.

Great is your reward. The woman in Mark received healing, but more importantly, she received spiritual wholeness. We can be physically healed and have no peace, but we can know peace of soul with or without physical healing.

MOMENTS TO REFLECT:

Desperation births faith. Faith touches the heart of God.

MOMENTS TO REFRESH:
Go *child, go. Touch the hem of His garment.* He is waiting for you.

MOMENTS TO REFOCUS:
Jesus loves you in your circumstances. He loves you even in a crowd.

MOMENTS TO RESPOND:
Faith births action. Choose to say, "Yes, Lord, I choose to obey Your still small voice. Your will be done."

Judy Myrick is an ordained minister with the Assemblies of God Southern Missouri District. A registered nurse since 1970, Myrick served as a certified registered nurse anesthetist from 1974 until her retirement in 1997. An endorsed Assemblies of God chaplain, in 2000 she became the first chaplain for the Hermann Area District Hospital in Hermann, Missouri, where she continues to serve.

Myrick has spoken at various conferences and functions and has made numerous ministry trips to Eastern Africa focusing on medical missions and evangelism. Her heart is to minister to people who have never heard the gospel, and to see people saved through the blood of Jesus, filled with the Holy Spirit, healed physically and emotionally, set free from bondages, and loosed to do the work of the Lord.

Contact Judy Myrick at: jamyrick@ktis.net.

CHAPTER 24

Broken and Undone

Tammy Oliver

A woman came with an alabaster jar of very expensive perfume, made of pure nard. She broke the jar and poured the perfume on [Jesus'] head.
Mark 14:3 (NIV)

A few years ago I was sitting in a workshop for pastors' wives. The speaker was talking about her encounter with the Lord and how she came to know Him in a more intimate way. As she was speaking, my spirit was screaming out, *God, I want to know You in that way. I am so hungry for more of Your presence!* That was a pivotal moment in my life. I left there determined to seek the Lord night after night, just to experience Him in a deeper way. For several months, my time with Him consisted of nothing but worship. I did not ask or want anything from Him. I simply desired to love Him for who He was, knowing that in the process, my life would be forever changed.

During this time, I began to really fall in love with Jesus. I would read about the woman who anointed Jesus and how she so "moved" Him with her worship. I would sit and pray, *"Lord, I want to move You like that with my worship."*

As the months passed my heart grew tender toward the Lord and all I wanted was to be a worshiper. I constantly prayed that He would teach me, use me, give me a heart like David, and anoint me to lead others into His presence. Oh, those are scary prayers! I didn't realize it at the time, but God can really only use "broken" and "undone" people. He can only use you to the extent you're willing to be broken.

Anyone in the Bible who was ever used of God first had to be broken. Moses was an educated, proud man who took it upon himself to kill an Egyptian. God had to send him to the back side of the desert for 40 years . . . to be broken. Peter said, "Lord, I will *never* deny You!" He had to be broken. Paul was an arrogant, hate-filled murderer. He had to be broken to be of any use to God. There was David, the man after God's own heart, who showed great brokenness and humility after being confronted with his own sin. And can you imagine the brokenness that Abraham experienced when God asked him to sacrifice his promised son, his most treasured, long-awaited possession?

Being broken has consequences. To find that place of usefulness to God is costly. To find that deeper place in His presence is not an easy road. Moses came away from God's presence with a mandate to speak for Him, despite a stuttering tongue; Jacob came away with a limp; Paul came away with a "thorn in the flesh." But now they were useful to God.

When I prayed to be a true worshiper, and to be used of God, I did not realize that I was about to endure the most painful months of my life. My husband and I dealt with personal issues, family issues, church issues, people issues (and any other issues you can imagine). All along I was crying out to God, "Why? How did this happen? When will it all be over?" I was even to the point of wanting to leave the ministry and go far away.

God has helped us to persevere, and as these times of difficulty finally begin to come to a close, I can look back and see that through every situation and every teardrop, the Lord was simply saying, *You're not broken enough; you're not totally surrendered . . . yet.* Please understand that I don't think that God is just sitting up in heaven plotting out pain and misery for each of us; but there is truly a cost. Jesus said it himself: "If anyone would come after me, he must deny himself and take up his cross and follow me" (Matthew 16:24). The cross not only represented a burden, but it represented death. So we can understand the fact that when Jesus was healing and doing miracles, the crowds were great, but when He began to speak of the "cost" of following Him, the crowds were not crowds at all.

I recently picked up my journal from two years ago. I had written about a particular evening that I had spent at an intercessory prayer meeting. That night as I prayed, I specifically felt the Lord say to me, *It's time for a new anointing.* I was excited about that and ready for it (or so I thought). Other things took place that night, but later on, I returned to prayer. Once again I felt the Lord say, *It's time for a new anointing.* After a short pause, it was as if He finished what He wanted to say, *It's time for a new anointing . . . but there's a price to pay.* I didn't really understand at the time what that price would be. (I was only hoping that it wouldn't be too great.) I've since realized that God is continually bringing me to a place of total brokenness and true desperation in order to be of use to Him. As a farmer has a season for breaking up unplowed ground, so God has seasons for breaking up the hardened or unplowed soil of our hearts.

The woman with the perfume took a painful journey through the glares and condemning words of those around her. She brought her most treasured possession and she *broke* it. As the fragrance filled the room, it was a sweet aroma of worship that Jesus said would forever be remembered.

The following song from my CD is a prayer each of us can pray:

Broken Spirit

I offer You a broken spirit
Dismantle every piece of pride
Releasing fragrance of my worship
Got nothin' more to hide

All I am and all I own
I lay crumbled at Your feet

So take the pieces of my brokenness
And feed the multitude
Take the vessel of my emptiness
One more time I offer You

— Tammy Oliver

MOMENTS TO REFLECT:

What are your most treasured possessions? Family?
Ministry? Dreams? Self? Can you honestly say that you
have yielded yourself to brokenness, offering every part
of your life for God's purposes, no matter the cost?

MOMENTS TO REFRESH:

"But he knows the way that I take; when he has tested
me, I will come forth as gold" (Job 23:10).

MOMENTS TO REFOCUS:

Brokenness does not mean that you are worthless. It
really means that you are priceless, and of greater value
in the hands of the Potter.

MOMENTS TO RESPOND:

"Jesus, I give You my most treasured possessions. I lay
all of the broken pieces of my life at Your feet. Just as
You had to break the bread to feed the multitudes, take
the pieces of my brokenness and use them for Your
glory."

Tammy Oliver *and her husband, Brent, pastor First Assembly of God in Delphi, Indiana. They pioneered the church in July 1990, and have watched God do incredible things in a small community. They have two children, Dustin and Cassidy. Tammy holds a bachelor of arts degree in music, and is the music/drama director and worship leader for their church. Her passion is to worship Jesus Christ and to continually lead the church body into His presence. Tammy released her first solo worship CD in December 2002.*

Contact Tammy Oliver (or to order her CD) at: toliver@firstag-delphi.org.

CHAPTER 25

The Fatherhood of God

Vicky L. Olsen

Yet, O Lord, you are our Father. We are the clay, you are the potter; we are all the work of your hand.
Isaiah 64:8 (NIV)

It is no secret that the father/daughter relationship is a special one in the life of a little girl. Dr. Benjamin Spock said, "By the time a girl is 4, she's apt to insist that she's going to marry her father when she grows up. She isn't clear just what marriage consists of, but she's absolutely sure who is the most important man in the world."[1]

Dr. James Dobson said, "A good father will leave his imprint on his daughter for the rest of her life."[2] What was your father like growing up? Did he teach you values, encourage you, provide for you, and protect you? Or was your relationship with your father nonexistent because of death, divorce, or desertion? Perhaps your father was physically in the home but emotionally detached from the rest of the family. Or maybe, like countless others, you lived in fear of your father because he was verbally, physically, or sexually abusive.

The relationship you had with your earthly father not only impacts the way you feel about yourself today, it also strongly affects the way you relate to your Heavenly Father. Correcting misconceptions about God will help you begin to comprehend the special relationship He wants to have with you.

Your Heavenly Father never ceases to be faithful. After I spoke on this topic at a women's retreat, a young housewife tearfully shared with me how long it took for her to forgive her father (who was divorced from her mother) for never showing up after promising time after time to come see her. Now a grandfather to her four children, he had recently called to tell them he would be paying them a visit.

Her 6-year-old daughter was so excited to see Grandpa she could hardly contain it and chattered nonstop about his upcoming arrival. "If my dad disappoints my daughter like he disappointed me," the woman said furiously, "I will be so mad at him I'll have to forgive him all over again."

The word "faithful" means dependable, reliable, or trustworthy. A person who is faithful is someone who keeps his promises. Your earthly father may not have done what he promised he would do, but God does.

Your Heavenly Father doesn't compare you with other people. Perhaps you were not musical or athletic, as your father would have wanted. You may have felt like you were a disappointment to your father because you were not studious enough or sociable enough. If your father criticized you on a regular basis, you most likely grew up with a low opinion of yourself. In his book *Healing for Damaged Emotions*, David Seamands explains that "low self-esteem is Satan's deadliest emotional and psychological weapon to bring defeat into your life. Low self-esteem paralyzes your potential."[3] God never intended for you to feel worthless, inadequate, or inferior.

God doesn't carry a grudge. Several years ago a woman in her early 30s shared with me that when she was a teenager she had almost succumbed to a sexual relationship with an older man she was dating at the time. Fortunately, she backed out before anything happened. Unbeknownst to her, however, someone had spotted her car at a local motel and promptly reported the incident to her father. This lovely lady has been happily married now for almost 15 years, has four beautiful children, and serves the Lord faithfully in ministry. Yet, her father takes almost every opportunity they are together to remind her of the time she disappointed him.

Do you have a father who won't let you forget mistakes you've made in the past? Does he keep reminding you of the time you let him down? If so, it will be hard for you to believe that your Heavenly Father really doesn't hold your past against you. Psalm 103:12 says, "As far as the east is from the west, so far has he removed our transgressions from us."

After my husband takes several pictures of the large catfish he catches, he dutifully tosses them back into the river. No, we do not fry them up for dinner. My husband lets them off the hook and sets them free. Do you need to let your father off the hook? Are you holding him responsible for your failures and frustrations? True forgiveness means to renounce, or let go, of our anger. Just as the fish are released back into the water, you can be released from the clutches of a bad father by forgiving him.

Ladies, what a comfort it should be to know that you are the daughter of a Father who accepts you just the way you are. And because of His inconceivable love, you *can* let go of your past.

MOMENTS TO REFLECT:
Think about your relationship with your earthly father. How has his influence (positive or negative) shaped who you are today?

MOMENTS TO REFRESH:
God's Word assures us of His love and fatherhood. "How great is the love the Father has lavished on us, that we should be called children of God!" (1 John 3:1).

MOMENTS TO REFOCUS:
Read Psalm 139:13-18. Allow God to heal your self-image and receive your self-esteem from His Word instead of your past.

MOMENTS TO RESPOND:

If you had a good father, take the time *today* to thank him for the positive impact he had on your life. My father went to be with the Lord in 1998 and not a day goes by that I don't wish I had one more opportunity to let him know how much he meant to me.

*As an experienced keynote speaker for a variety of audiences, **Vicky L. Olsen** has motivated and inspired hundreds to live whole and meaningful lives. Vicky travels nationally as a Christian conference speaker and personality trainer and has also equipped ministry leaders nationwide to communicate skillfully and confidently with her "Speaking for His Glory" seminar.*

Vicky and her husband, Rick, are the founders of Christian V.I.E.W. (Vessels of Influence, Excellence, & Wholeness) Ministries. In addition to being a contributing author to two books, Vicky is in her third year of writing a bi-monthly column for Woman's Touch *magazine. In 2002, at the age of 39, Vicky gave birth to their first child, Abby Rose, who often accompanies her mom to speaking events.*

Contact Vicky Olsen at: www.VickyOlsen.com.

CHAPTER 26

First, You Forgive

Kathleen Parker

And be kind to one another, tenderhearted, forgiving one another, even as God in Christ forgave you.
Ephesians 4:32 (NKJV)

Monday, March 4, 2002—the day my life changed forever.

My husband and I sat across from each other at the small table in our fifth-wheel trailer. Ken had been released from the hospital a few days earlier and I had prepared one of his favorite breakfasts—waffles and bacon. We were full-time RVers in a volunteer church building ministry. We were doing what we loved most, and felt privileged to be able to serve God this way. "Here am I! Send me" was the Scripture from Isaiah that became the theme for our lives. God had equipped Ken from his youth with the knowledge and skill to build just about anything, from furniture and cabinets to houses and churches. And now that we were officially retired, Ken's greatest desire was to build churches, and mine was to be by his side. But Ken's life had already changed forever.

We sat quietly, each immersed in our own thoughts. My mind raced back and forth between the past, present, and the uncertain future. It had all happened so fast—the excruciating headaches, the doctor appointment, the hurried CT scan, the black films on the light board showing a huge white lump—a brain tumor.

I was brought back to the present by the touch of Ken taking my hand in his. I looked up and smiled at the man I loved so dearly. White gauze bandages concealed the 46 staples in his skull. "There's something I have to tell you." His voice was sad and serious.

My stomach muscles tightened as I braced myself and asked, "What?"

He looked down, hesitated, then said, "I was unfaithful to you."

"What?" I burst into tears as my mind reeled. "Who? When? How could you?" In that instant of shock and disbelief I felt as though life itself was being sucked out of me.

"I'm sorry. I'm so sorry. I love you so much. Please forgive me," he pleaded. We cried together for a long time and a part of me died that day.

I spent the night crying and asking God, "Why? Why did this happen? And why did I have to know?"

For the next two weeks my mind and my body seemed to shut down. I couldn't eat; I couldn't sleep. All I could do was cry. Ken asked me again, "Can you forgive me?" He knew that it was against God that he had sinned, and from God he had to receive forgiveness. And I knew it, too. I remembered the hours he had spent weeping and praying at the altar, his faithfulness in reading God's Word every day, his readiness to share God's love and grace with the unsaved, his servant's heart. God had forgiven Ken—a long time before. Now I could do no less.

"Yes, Ken, I forgive you." And I had. I moved that horrible revelation to the back recesses of my mind and did my best to keep it there.

The six months following surgery became a routine of doctors, radiation, chemotherapy, MRI's and CT scans. We did everything humanly possible to keep Ken alive. Hundreds of Christians across the country prayed for his healing. But on September 13, seven months after the diagnosis, Ken left his earthly body and took up residence with the King of kings.

After the funeral, as the indescribable loneliness settled in, I began to sink into a dreadful, incapacitating depression. I had to force myself to do the most mundane tasks. Satan went to work overtime on my mind. I was on an emotional roller coaster of grief, despair, guilt, humiliation, loneliness and pain. The man I had loved for more than 27 years, who introduced me to Jesus, who helped raise my two sons, was gone and his death and betrayal were like a double-edged sword piercing my heart. "How much pain can one person endure, Lord?" I wrote in my journal on October 10. On October 13 I wrote, "The loneliness is dreadful. It is cold and dark and awful. God, please break through and touch me. Hold me and heal this pain, Lord. Please turn the light back on."

Three days later I wrote these words to Jesus: "Only You can fill this empty place in my heart. Only You, only You." And later that evening, "Only You can bring quiet peace to my tormented soul and make me whole." Within a few days the Lord had given me the words to the song that began the healing process. This song, "Only You," ministered to me day and night for weeks. Psalm 42:8 says, "The Lord will command His lovingkindness in the day-time, and in the night His song *shall be* with me—a prayer to the God of my life." The Lord gave me another song, and another. Each one a balm of healing for my mind and emotions. Songs of praise and worship; songs about His grace and mercy and love. My prayer time on the way to and from work became my time to hear from God through songs. I frequently pulled off the road to write them down. Psalm 40:1-3 describes perfectly what God has been doing in my life: "I waited patiently for the Lord; and He inclined to me, and heard my cry. He also brought me up out of a horrible pit, out of the miry clay, and set my feet upon a rock, *and* established my steps. He has put a new song in my mouth—praise to our God; many will see *it* and fear, and will trust in the Lord." God is resurrecting that part of me that had died—He is restoring my joy.

I've learned many lessons over the past year and a half. First, you forgive. Oswald Chambers wrote, "When we have experienced the unfathomable forgiveness of God for all our wrong, we must exhibit that same forgiveness to others." I've learned that forgiveness must be immediate; healing is a process. Just as a wound heals from the inside out, the healing of a wounded spirit takes time, cannot be rushed, and the scar will eventually fade. I understand better the sovereignty of God. One day I was presenting God with a long list of whys—"Why did Ken have to die? Why was he unfaithful to me? Why did he even tell me?" God gently spoke to my heart, *This is My business. I am God.* In that moment the sovereignty of God became clear to me. It truly is none of my business what He chooses to do or how He chooses to do it; what He allows or doesn't allow. If I say He is Lord of my life, I must give Him all of my life. I have learned that Jesus is sufficient. He is all I need.

MOMENTS TO REFLECT:

God has the power to heal and restore broken hearts and broken lives. You can assist this process by reflecting more on blessings than on hurts.

MOMENTS TO REFRESH:

The presence of God brings times of refreshing (see Acts 3:19). His Word refreshes, blesses and encourages. He is the God of new beginnings and fresh starts.

MOMENTS TO REFOCUS:

Don't dwell on the past. Live in the present. Look to the future. God will transform you by the renewing of your mind (Romans 12:2).

MOMENTS TO RESPOND:

Commit your life to God each day. Worship Him in prayer and song. Say to the Lord, "Here am I! Send me."

Kathleen Parker has ministered through drama in more than 40 churches, district councils and women's retreats. She has produced and directed numerous cantatas and plays, including a full-length children's play and several skits. More recently, the Lord has inspired her to write more than 20 songs and praise choruses and she is currently working on a children's musical. She has been a featured speaker at women's retreats and has ministered in convalescent hospitals. Kathleen now lives in Indianapolis, Indiana, where she is a member of Calvary Temple. She has two sons and four stepchildren.

Contact Kathleen Parker at: kathleen.parker@sbcglobal.net.

To Give Is Christ

Ruth Puleo

Freely (without pay) you have received,
freely (without charge) give.
Matthew 10:8 (Amplified)

I had spent hours forging through the holiday crowds at an overpopulated, understaffed shopping mall to find the appropriate gifts for our children. Their carefully selected wish lists had been my guide. Each gift was secretly transported to my bedroom, wrapped speedily and placed around the Christmas tree before the children had a chance to get a premature look.

In the flurry of Christmas morning our tribe devoured an eggs-and-pancakes breakfast, shared the reading of the Christmas story and assembled themselves for our annual family gift distribution ritual. What had taken hours to

locate, select and wrap only took minutes to open. My
husband was summoned for the task of erecting each toy
before it could be utilized. To our dismay, we found our
children gleefully occupied for the remainder of the day
playing house in the boxes that their gifts once graced. It
dawned on me that the value of a gift is determined by the
recipient and to be truly appreciated it must be utilized.

It is hard to imagine that just a few months ago I experienced the heaviness of depression for the first time in my
life. I have always been a positive, optimistic person who
loved life and faced each challenge with the belief that God
would see me through. My earliest memories as a child
were ones of prayer and fellowship with my Heavenly
Father following the example set before me by my parents.
After completing Bible college training, I met the man of
my dreams, married, followed a call to ministry and raised
three children in the parsonage. Our son and oldest daughter are in the process of preparing for ministry overseas.
But our youngest daughter, Julie, while still living at home
and attending high school, was stricken with migraine
headaches that have ravaged her life continuously for two
and a half years.

Julie was the leader of our youth worship team and
developing her gifts for a future in music ministry. We followed all of the scriptural admonitions to those who are
sick. We prayed. We fasted. Our church prayed and fasted,
too. We traveled to ministries for special prayer. We read.
We studied. We remained faithful in our work for God.
Julie was examined by many doctors and tried many medications that did not work and in most cases made it worse
by the complicating side effects. After two years without
any improvement, she prayerfully decided to withdraw

from all of the medications that were prescribed. In that five-month process, her health worsened, her migraines increased and her spirit encountered overwhelming discouragement. Having always been the rescuing mom, the one who "made it all better," I found it difficult to watch her health and hope decline without being personally affected.

During my darkest hour, when it felt as though no one was hearing my prayers, God unwrapped His priceless gifts before my eyes. I saw the panoramic view of salvation—unconditional mercy and love. Christ suffered more than physical pain on the cross, He suffered separation from His Heavenly Father as He bore all of my sins so that I could have complete forgiveness and the hope of eternal life. "For God so greatly loved and dearly prized the World that he [even] gave up His only begotten (unique) Son, so that whoever believes in (trusts in, clings to, relies on) Him shall not perish (come to destruction, be lost) but have eternal (everlasting) life" (John 3:16). From a child, I had experienced God's love. But, for the first time in my life, I recognized that there was nothing I could do to earn it, God simply loved me because I was His creation and it was in His heart to do so.

With this new revelation of God's love, I began seeing people around me differently—I saw them through the loving eyes of our Savior. God has challenged me to minister to hurting women and He is bringing healing where there was once pain. "Give thanks to the Lord, for he is good! His faithful love endures forever. Has the Lord redeemed you? Then speak out! Tell others he has saved you" (Psalm 107:1,2, NLT).

Sometimes other people have to assist us in unwrapping our gifts if we are struggling in the process. God sent someone to Julie to remind her that even though she could not control her pain, she could control her future with God's help. "For I know the thoughts and plans that I have for you, says the Lord, thoughts and plans for welfare and peace and not for evil, to give you hope in your final outcome" (Jeremiah 29:11, Amplified). Julie made a decision to act upon her faith and apply to Bible college. She completed her home school requirements for high school in spite of her pain. She made a decision to celebrate life and the opportunity that God had placed before her. Julie was accepted at the Bible college and is making plans to prepare for a music ministry.

Mary, the mother of Jesus, gave praise to her Lord even though she did not know what her future would hold. "My soul magnifies and extols the Lord, and my spirit rejoices in God my Savior . . . For He Who is almighty has done great things for me" (Luke 1:46,47,49). God has given us a future and a hope, let's give Him a sacrifice of praise.

My children contentedly played with a box on Christmas Day, not realizing the value of what it once contained. I pray that Christ will enable us to unwrap the gifts of salvation—His unconditional love and the hope of our future in Him—so that we can share those gifts with everyone we meet. "Freely (without pay) you have received, freely (without charge) give" (Matthew 10:8).

MOMENTS TO REFLECT:

What are some of the best gifts you have received that were not "things"?

MOMENTS TO REFRESH:

Despite any challenges you may be faced with, God loves you. Look at the opportunities God has placed in your life and celebrate life.

MOMENTS TO REFOCUS:

Look at both your blessings and your trials. Focus on the fact that Jesus is with you in both.

MOMENTS TO RESPOND:

Give thanks to the Lord for all the blessings in your life.

Ruth Puleo is Women's Ministries director for the Pennsylvania-Delaware District of the Assemblies of God. An ordained minister, she also serves as a pastor on staff with her husband, John, who is the senior pastor of Christian Life Assembly in Stroudsburg, Pennsylvania.

Ruth was raised in a minister's home and came to know the Lord at a very young age. She attended Zion Bible Institute and Northwest College. She has ministered in many churches, retreats and conventions locally and nationally and travels overseas ministering in Bible schools and at churches, to nationals and national pastors' wives.

Ruth has a heart for souls and especially for the needs of women. She believes in the necessity of intercessory prayer and exercises that in her life and ministry. Ruth is the mother of three children, all serving the Lord.

Contact Ruth Puleo at: rpuleo@ptd.net.

CHAPTER 28

When It Seems Hopeless . . .

See the Hope and Not the Less

Karen C. Rydwansky

We wait in hope for the Lord; he is our help and our shield. In him our hearts rejoice, for we trust in his holy name. May your unfailing love rest upon us, O Lord, even as we put our hope in you.
Psalm 33:20-22 (NIV)

When my husband and I were married we looked forward to the day we could start our family and enjoy the blessings of our own children. However, that dream had to be put on hold as my husband was called to duty in Vietnam. But we had our plan, one year in Vietnam and then we'd start our family. But life doesn't always go according to our plans. You never consider that there's going to be a problem. Five years went by and still no baby.

In those days you didn't talk about problems with conceiving. Those matters were private and not to be shared. People assumed that no children meant a purposeful decision not to have children. "What, no baby yet?" or "Don't be self-centered; you should have a baby" were some of the hurtful comments made to me. Attending baby showers was especially painful.

We endured the indignity of fertility tests and I consented to taking fertility drugs. Those were the early days when fertility drugs were unproven and often reaped disastrous results. Babies without fingers and arms, or with other deformities, made drug therapy very risky. But our desire for a child overrode the risks involved.

Finally, the joyful day came when I conceived, only to have our hopes dashed as we lost the baby at the end of the third month. Again, no one knew and so we sorrowed alone.

The first Sunday back at church there was a baby dedication. As the pastor began to pray over the baby I had to get up and walk out because the tears were streaming down my face. Proverbs 13:12 tells us that "hope deferred makes the heart sick, but a longing fulfilled is a tree of life." Our hearts were sick with sorrow and it seemed our longings would never be fulfilled. When hopes are dashed and there seems to be only silence from heaven, what do you do? How long do you continue to believe that God will bring an answer to your prayers? Was this really God's will for our lives?

Hopelessness comes when we see more "less" than "hope." Hannah was in that situation as Peninnah bore child after child while Hannah remained barren. Rather than encourage Hannah to hope in God, Peninnah ridiculed and mocked Hannah's barrenness. Even the love of a doting husband could never fill Hannah's empty arms. When life is "hopeLESS" there is only one thing to do—pray to the Lord, our only source of hope. Hannah cried out in her bitterness and sorrow. Everyone around her misunderstood her actions, but she kept crying out to God, and in God's perfect timing Samuel was born (1 Samuel 1).

Hope has to be rooted in God's timing. Samuel's birth came at the perfect time for Israel. The priesthood had miserably failed and the Word of God was rarely heard, but God raised up Samuel to be His voice—in time to anoint Israel's first king, Saul, and then to anoint David. God's timing is always perfect. When it seems "hopeless," we need more than ever to hope in God. He will turn our situation around in His perfect timing.

Simeon and Anna had to wait for God's promise to be fulfilled in a hopeless situation. They knew that God had promised a Savior, One who would come and set His people free. What if they had given up waiting and hoping? What if they had just gotten too busy with their own lives and skipped the place of worship? What if they had allowed the hopelessness of their situation to dim the promise that a Child would be born that would set the people free? They would have missed seeing Jesus. But they did not let the long years of waiting dim their hope. Their hope kept them in the place of worship and prayer. Finally, their hope was turned to reality. Hope triumphed as Simeon held Jesus in his arms. Hope rang with the praises of God as Anna recognized that the redemption of Israel had come (Luke 2).

Sometimes it seems as though God has forgotten. But God never forgets us. God will always reward the faithfulness of those who wait patiently in hope. When David felt discouraged and downcast, he put his hope in God knowing that God is always faithful (Psalm 42:5,11; 43:5). Hope will never disappoint us, because of God's love poured out into our hearts by the Holy Spirit (Romans 5:5).

Don't give up! When you least expect a miracle, God will act. Keep believing; He has not forgotten you; He will fulfill His plans for you (Psalm 33:11). After almost seven years of waiting our first child, Kristen was born and laid in my arms. The gift of her life was worth the wait and her coming changed our lives forever. In time, two other girls were born into our family and now a granddaughter. Our arms and hearts are full.

MOMENTS TO REFLECT:

I can confidently trust God's plan and His timing for my life. "'For I know the plans I have for you,' declares the Lord, 'plans to prosper you and not to harm you, plans to give you *hope* and a future'" (Jeremiah 29:11).

MOMENTS TO REFRESH:

When I am weary of the waiting and feel it is hope**less**, I have new strength as I put **more** hope in the Lord.

"Even youths grow tired and weary, and young men stumble and fall; but those who *hope* in the Lord will renew their strength. They will soar on wings like eagles; they will run and not grow weary, they will walk and not be faint" (Isaiah 40:30,31).

MOMENTS TO REFOCUS:

I can have joy and patience as I pray in faith believing my hope will be rewarded. "Be joyful in *hope*, patient in affliction, faithful in prayer" (Romans 12:12).

MOMENTS TO RESPOND:

I will continue to praise God, for my *hope* is in Him who is worthy of all praise. "But as for me, I will always have *hope*; I will praise you more and more" (Psalm 71:14).

Karen C. Rydwansky is ordained with the Assemblies of God and was recently appointed as a church planter for the Southern New England District. She is pastoring Crossroads Worship Center in Weymouth, Massachusetts, with her husband, Frank, who is the administrator of a private Christian school. They have three daughters and a granddaughter.

Karen served as a district director of Women's Ministries for six years and during that time served on the National Women's Ministries Committee. She was featured in the Pentecostal Evangel *in the article "Role Models: Women Touching the World" (February 28, 1999).*

She served on the board of Teen Challenge and is presently on the trustee board of Zion Bible Institute, Barrington, Rhode Island.

Karen was associate pastor of Glad Tidings Church, Quincy, Massachusetts, where she learned to embrace and master cross-cultural ministry. She ministers at retreats, worship seminars and meetings for women and girls in many districts and uses visual illustrations as "The Classy Bag Lady" to bring biblical truth to life. She is attending Gordon-Conwell Seminary, Center for Urban Ministries Education (CUME) in Boston, pursuing an M.Div. She enjoys playing string bass with symphonic groups as time allows.

Contact Karen Rydwansky at: Kcryd@aol.com.

My Soul Remembers

Mary Selzer

My soul still remembers and sinks within me.
This I recall to my mind, therefore I have hope.
Lamentations 3:20,21(NKJV)

No one enjoys growing older. The aches. The pains. The slower pace. The frustration of a body that can't keep up with the mind. Or the mind that can't keep up with the body. The fear of lost independence.

Aging is inevitable. This frail body can handle only so much for so long. But for children of God there is an indescribable inner sustenance through His Spirit that supersedes the weakness of the flesh.

My mother's bout with Alzheimer's brought this truth home to me. Let me start from the beginning.

My Iranian grandparents arranged my parents' marriage in 1936 and, at the age of 18, my mother settled down to housekeeping and child raising. A new church had been planted in the neighborhood and a woman named Lu Adiska invited my older sister to Sunday School. My mother consented, and within a short time she began to attend as well.

During an illness, my mother called for the pastor to pray for her and she was instantly healed. When my father returned from work later that day, he found my mother performing her normal household chores, completely well. He was so impressed that he began to attend church and gave his heart to the Lord.

Lu Adiska took my mother under her wing and began to visit her regularly. As my mother related it, the first time she visited, she sat in a chair and sighed deeply while saying, "Wonderful Jesus."

My mother was in awe. "They were the most beautiful words I had ever heard," she told me. "I determined right there that whatever spirit Lu Adiska had in her I wanted in me. It flowed so naturally from her and I wanted the same thing to flow from me."

For years, my mother remained very active in the church, teaching teens, mentoring young wives, ministering to widows, caring for babies—whatever needed to be done, she did it. The love that flowed from her attracted numerous people. She listened. She loved. She prayed.

In the early 1990s, we learned that my mother had Alzheimer's disease. It was in the fairly early stages, but it was still a devastating shock to our family and to the church. As the disease progressed, she slowly lost her independence and, eventually, it became necessary for someone to be with her at all times. When she wandered off a couple of times, we feared for her safety and made the decision to move her into an Alzheimer's assisted-living unit.

In her new home, the caregivers do their best to help the residents maintain their independence and dignity, keeping them active for several hours a day. I think of one resident who, no matter what else she was wearing—pajamas, sweat pants, slacks, or a dress—would always wear a blazer and carry a purse. Then, she would sit near the dining room and wait for the lunch cart. When lunch arrived, she announced that it was time to eat and began giving orders to the other residents. When I inquired about her former employment, I learned that she had been an administrative assistant in a large law firm and was used to taking charge. Another sweet lady dramatically cried every day for her nephew. She would throw the back of her hand over her forehead and moan for him, or with great deliberation would weep as she laid her head on the dining room table, making sure everyone at the table could see and hear her. One day I asked her what type of work she had done. Proudly, she stated, "I was a drama teacher."

And then, there's my mother. Almost as soon as she moved into the facility, her ministry-oriented mind kicked in and she became a comfort to confused and distressed residents. She would hug and kiss them, whispering, "God loves you." Almost immediately, their distress would cease.

The disease has now progressed to the point where she can barely put two words together; but there remains a rich spirit of love and comfort about her that still draws people. She has a brilliant smile and shining eyes. That which is deep within her spirit is so much greater than the frailty of her mind and body.

The Lord recently reminded me that He had indeed answered my mother's prayer. For now, what her mind cannot do, her heart does automatically. It is no longer she that lives, but Christ that lives within her (Galatians 2:20).

MOMENTS TO REFLECT:

Do you fear the aging process? Are you struggling to keep what God has intended should naturally fade away? This body and mind may fade, but His eternal Spirit, with all of its power and richness, will remain alive within you (James 4:14; Ecclesiastes 12:7).

MOMENTS TO REFRESH:

Remember that God knew before you were born exactly how long you would live. And He intends for every day to be rich in Him. He *does* have a future and a hope for you (Psalm 139; Jeremiah 29:11,12).

MOMENTS TO REFOCUS:

According to Galatians 2:20, this life is lived by faith. Whether you are in the best of health or the worst of health—whether you are in the first years or the latter years—you live by faith (Hebrews 12:2).

MOMENTS TO RESPOND:

Read Lamentations 3:20-26. Be encouraged as you sing: "Great is Thy faithfulness, O God my Father; There is no shadow of turning with Thee; Thou changest not, Thy compassions, they fail not; As Thou hast been, Thou forever will be. Great is Thy faithfulness! Great is Thy faithfulness! Morning by morning new mercies I see. All I have needed Thy hand hath provided; Great is Thy faithfulness, Lord unto me!"[1]

Mary Selzer has served as the Michigan District Women's Ministries director since 1998 and has been involved with Women's Ministries for 14 years. She served a two-year term on the National Committee for Women's Ministries and currently is on the Publications Advisory Board for Woman's Touch *magazine and on the Advisory Committee for Touch With Hope, a ministry to single mothers.*

A credentialed minister with the Assemblies of God, Mary received a B.A. degree in religious education from Central Bible College, Springfield, Missouri, and a B.S. in business administration from St. Mary of the Woods College, Terre Haute, Indiana. Her husband, Louis, pastors in Eastpointe, Michigan, where Mary leads the choir and teaches one of the adult Sunday School classes. Prior to entering pastoral ministry, the Selzers served on staff at Mid-America Teen Challenge, Cape Girardeau, Missouri, for several years.

The Selzers have two daughters, Rachel and Sarah.

Contact Mary Selzer at: intouch10@juno.com.

CHAPTER 30

Memories for a Lifetime

⌒

Lillian Sparks

*By wisdom a house is built, and through
understanding it is established; through knowledge its
rooms are filled with rare and beautiful treasures.
Proverbs 24:3,4 (NIV)*

It happened one Sunday morning. My husband was the
senior pastor of a large church in Ohio and had called all
the children to come down front for a mini-sermon. He
wanted to emphasize God's plan for their lives and, therefore, posed this question: "What do you want to be when
you grow up?" One after another, the children responded,
"An astronaut . . . a fireman . . . a doctor . . . a singer . . .
a teacher."

Four-year-old, unpredictable Jenell sat directly in front of her father, wildly waving her hand in his face like a windshield wiper on a rainy day. When all of the others had been recognized, he had no other recourse than to acknowledge this bubbly youngster.

"Yes, Jenell. What do you want to be when you grow up?" Without even a moment's hesitation, she blurted out, "Just a plain old, ordinary mom . . . like my mother!" This in spite of my rigorous speaking schedule, authoring of two books, and international travels, which had for the most part been unnoticed by our children. To Jenell, I was just a plain old, ordinary mom. What a great compliment!

Someone has written, "Who we are, what we become, depends largely on those who love us." How true. When you were a kid, certain people were there who made a lasting impression upon your life. They were the people who taught you something about life you have never forgotten. No matter where you grew up—small rural community or large urban area—the people on your list had a tremendous influence on you. They helped shape and mold your life and dreams. Someday you will be on someone's list.

A family has been described as a museum of memories. How wonderful to build memories that will last forever, and how quickly our opportunity of influence will pass.

Solomon, in the two simple-sounding verses above, tells us what we need to transform our house into a home.

By wisdom a house is built. It is wise parents who build their home on godly principles and strong biblical teaching. When children are small, show them by example the value of prayer, Bible reading, faithful church attendance, and tithing. Proverbs 22:6 tells us, "Train a child in the way he should go, and when he is old he will not turn from it." In other words, give your children a heart for God!

One of my favorite stories is about 5-year-old Johnny, who rebelliously refused to wash his hands until Mom threatened him with a spanking. Stretching to reach the sink, hands lathered to the hilt, Mom overheard Johnny: "Jesus and germs, Jesus and germs, that's all I ever hear around here, and I haven't seen either one of them yet!"

Through understanding it is established. Understanding is seeing with insight or, we might say, reading between the lines. As parents, we quickly learn that it is as important to listen to what is not being said as to what is said. True understanding goes beyond surface level and emotional responses, to hear what is in the heart. We must learn not to be defensive or to take every comment personally. What are they really trying to say? Are they hurting, feeling rejection, or experiencing frustration? Solomon gives us sound advice in Proverbs 2:3,5, "If you call out for insight and cry aloud for understanding . . . then you will understand the fear of the Lord and find the knowledge of God."

Through knowledge its rooms are filled with . . . treasures. What are the rare and beautiful treasures that will fill the rooms in our house? These are memories that will last for a lifetime—memories of holidays, celebrations, family vacations, accomplishments, answered prayers, and humorous experiences. These are the moments in life that make us laugh and make us cry.

Moving is always a traumatic time for a family. In November 1998 when our family moved from North Huntingdon, Pennsylvania, to Springfield, Missouri, we decided to make a memory. Knowing how difficult it would be to say good-bye to our house on 14400 Jonathan Drive, we thought of a creative way to ease the pain.

The day before the moving van arrived, we took a portable cassette recorder from room to room and allowed each family member to share their favorite memories. From bedrooms to kitchen, from family room to bathrooms, we recorded six years of laughter and tears that we had shared together. The hardest place was the living room where we said farewell to our oldest son, Bryon, when he went to heaven.

Edith Schaeffer, in her book *What Is a Family?*, devotes her longest chapter to the idea that a family is a "perpetual relay of truth." It is a place where principles are hammered and shaped on the anvil of everyday living, where character traits are sculptured under the watchful eyes of moms and dads. The relay place—a race with a hundred batons. Paul said, "Run with patience the race that is set before us."

I like what Schaeffer says: "Occasionally, God gives a family a memory that becomes so deep a crease in the brain . . . time can never erase it." God can give your family memories that will last a lifetime!

MOMENTS TO REFLECT:

"Who we are, what we become, depends largely on those who love us." Who were the people who taught you something about life that you have never forgotten?

MOMENTS TO REFRESH:

Someone has said, "Our minds have forgotten what our hearts still remember." What kind of memories do you want to leave behind for those you love?

MOMENTS TO REFOCUS:

How can we be a "perpetual relay of truth" to the next generation?

MOMENTS TO RESPOND:

How can we build memories into people's lives?

Lillian Sparks has served as national Women's Ministries director for the Assemblies of God and editor of Woman's Touch *magazine. She has also worked with WorldServe and as a Christian education director, college music professor, kindergarten teacher and a retreat and seminar speaker, traveling extensively both nationally and internationally. She is the author of two books:* Tough Cookie *and* Parents Cry Too. *Lillian and her husband, Steve, have three children. She resides in Springfield, Missouri.*

Contact Lillian Sparks at: slljb5sparks@cs.com.

CHAPTER 31

Experiencing the Amazing

Vicki Strickland

*Consecrate yourselves, for tomorrow the Lord will
do amazing things among you.*
Joshua 3:5 (NIV)

The Book of Joshua teaches us many things. The
Children of Israel were right on the banks of the Jordan
River, viewing the much-anticipated Promised Land before
them. I wonder if they thought this day would ever come.
Joshua had been appointed by God to be the leader after
Moses' death, to take the Children of Israel into the ful-
fillment of the promise.

As this new leader spent time with God seeking direction, the Lord instructed Joshua to tell the people,
"Consecrate yourselves, for tomorrow the Lord will do
amazing things among you" (Joshua 3:5). After this time

of consecration, they crossed the Jordan River and finally, after years of wandering in the desert, they arrived in the Promised Land.

What disappointment must have surged through them when they realized that the very first battle to be fought in this new land was the city of Jericho—one of the most fortified cities ever built! The Lord sent an angel to give Joshua some pretty unusual instructions that, if followed, would bring down the walls of the city without force. Joshua shared these instructions with the people and they moved out to carry out the plans of the Lord. As promised, the walls came down and Jericho was delivered into their hands. The Lord accomplished this incredible task in such a way that there was no way the Israelites could take the credit.

Much of their success hinged on obedience to those words in Joshua 3:5. What did this mean for the Israelites and what does it mean for your life today? In this account, consecration included circumcision, which is a time of cutting away unnecessary flesh (see Joshua 5). In our lives it is also necessary to remove the unnecessary fleshly parts. Since consecration is followed by the Lord doing "amazing" things, then what is the "amazing"?

The Lord answered this question for me in a few very special and definite ways. As I was commuting to work one day, along the freeway there was a large field full of bright yellow flowers. The sun shining on the flowers made them glow. I thanked the Lord for His handiwork and His beauty. He spoke to my heart, saying, *Vicki, this is the amazing.*

A few months later my family vacationed in Alaska. We took a plane ride around Mt. McKinley. The sights were mind blowing. The white of the snow resembled giant marshmallows and the blue waters of the glaciers were the bluest I've ever seen. Up there soaring with the eagles, again I thanked God for His handiwork and again I sensed Him say, *Vicki, this is the amazing.*

Later we went on a glacier cruise. Our boat brought us close to glaciers that were hundreds of years old, hundreds of feet thick and an incredible blue. Again the Lord said, *Vicki, this is the amazing.*

After returning home, I spent a season asking the Lord what He was trying to tell me. Very clearly I heard, *The amazing, Vicki, is that thing that you cannot create on your own.* I'd love to be able to share with friends our Mt. McKinley experience, but that's not possible. I could not recreate the mountain in my living room.

The Lord showed me that He desires to do "the amazing" in me, that He wants to do through me what I cannot accomplish on my own. If the time of consecration released the amazing for the Israelites, then consecration will release the amazing in my life as well. If I allow the Lord to cut away the unnecessary, the areas that don't bring Him glory, then He will be released to work in, and through, my life in ways that will be as extraordinary as the walls of Jericho falling.

We come to the altar of consecration many times throughout our lives. We must make the commitment to always allow the Lord to strip away the unnecessary from our lives.

The Lord has sent us to be His messengers to touch a lost and dying world. As consecration released the amazing, the supernatural, for the Children of Israel, so will our consecration release the supernatural in our lives. Isaiah 40:3 challenges us to prepare a way in the desert for our Lord. The goal is that the Jesus who lives in us will walk into the lives of those around us. Unfortunately, there are times when the Lord finds issues in our lives in His way—fear, insecurities, unforgiveness, and others. There are areas He has repeatedly asked us to consecrate and give to Him . . . day after day and year after year. This world is looking for the supernatural, for the amazing. They are hoping that there is something, someone larger than their problems that can help them through life. Too often in my life the Lord has sent me into places to minister His hope and love and, because of the time it took for Him to deal with my issues, the opportunity has passed and a life has gone untouched.

What are those areas that the Lord has been speaking to you about? What does He want you to put on the altar of consecration? Is it an attitude, your thought life, past failures, past hurts? Perhaps it's fear, doubt or insecurity. In what area of your life do you long to see the supernatural? Ask the Lord to bring to your mind those areas, those things. Lay them before Him today. Seek His forgiveness, His healing power and step fully into the promise of restoration. Ask the Lord to accomplish the supernatural through your life and to do it just like He did with the Israelites—in such a way that you will not be able to take the credit.

MOMENTS TO REFLECT:

What is an area of your life that God has been asking for? What has been holding you back from giving it to Him?

MOMENTS TO REFRESH:

Take time to look for the amazing that is all around you.

MOMENTS TO REFOCUS:

What are you afraid of? Are you willing to give that fear to Jesus?

MOMENTS TO RESPOND:

What steps will you take today to release the amazing in your life? To whom will you be accountable for these changes?

Vicki Strickland is the Oregon District Women's Ministries director for the Assemblies of God. She was raised in a home missions church in Arizona, where her parents ministered to the White Mountain Apache Indians. She served as the Women's Ministries coordinator for her local church for five years, pioneering a ministry that impacted the community as well as the church. She served as Central Oregon's Women's Ministries sectional representative for two years.

Vicki has a strong desire to help women reach their fullest potential and impact those they come in contact with. She has ministered to women at conferences and retreats throughout the Northwest, and in Swaziland, Jordan, Egypt, and Greece. She and her husband, Randy, have one daughter, Randi.

Contact Vicki Strickland at:
vicki.strickland@oregonag.com.

CHAPTER 32

Starting Over

Priscilla Wilson Taylor

*Not that I speak in regard to need, for I have learned in
whatever state I am, to be content.*
Philippians 4:11 (NKJV)

"I have never loved you. Our marriage has been a mistake!" With those words from my husband's lips, life as I knew it was over. Nothing would ever be the same. After 23 years of marriage I was single again. My future seemed a dark, empty void filled with questions and foreboding. Rejected . . . all of my plans and dreams for the future were shattered. All that was left was my faith in God.

How do you begin again? How do you pick up the pieces of your life? Where do you start? In the midst of that confusion I read, "Be anxious for nothing, but in everything by prayer and supplication, with thanksgiving, let your requests be made known to God; and the peace of God, which surpasses all understanding, will guard your hearts and minds through Christ Jesus" (Philippians 4:6,7). The exciting news is that the peace did come!

On my first day alone, I awoke to the reality that life had changed, only to realize that the melody going around in my head was "Jesus loves me, this I know." What a great God! He let me know that, although I felt unloved, I was truly loved by the Prince of Peace. The simple song I had sung as a child became my lifeline and I held on tightly!

Have you been there? Have you had tragedy strike and wonder how you will get through the day? Can you hear the music? Jesus loves you, too! Take His hand. He will walk with you through your crisis, no matter how alone you may feel.

Living in a sinful world will at some point bring most of us into some kind of crisis. Bad things happen to good people—sometimes due to our own poor choices, at other times due to undeserved tragedy out of our control. How you respond to that pain and disappointment is up to you. It's much easier to talk about forgiveness than to forgive, but it is your choice. You may choose to nurse your hurt and guard your pain, or you may give it to the Lord.

Start by following Paul's advice: "Whatever things are true, whatever things *are* noble, whatever things *are* just, whatever things *are* pure, whatever things *are* lovely, whatever things *are* of good report, if *there is* any virtue and if *there is* anything praiseworthy—meditate on these things" (Philippians 4:8). It's a choice! Instead of thinking about how you were wronged, find something that is lovely, some nugget of good news that can take your mind off your situation. It's up to you. Psychologists tell us that positive thinking will make us happier, more successful and fulfilled.

Time on your hands is deadly when you are by yourself and hurting. Left alone you rehearse the pain you feel and any hurt is magnified many times over. That is the time to get up and go to work. In my house there were always dresser drawers to be cleaned, a kitchen floor that needed waxing or, maybe just a warm cup of tea and a good book to get lost in. You can allow yourself to stew in self-pity or you can give the pain to Jesus and get on with life. Begin with forgiveness and the awareness that your situation is no surprise to Him.

There are many who need your love and concern. Reach out to them, and you'll soon find that you are not alone. As simplistic as it sounds, it really works. The God of peace has promised!

Contentment is another choice to be made. My son was 3 months old when we took a staff position at a large church out of state. While waiting for our home, we lived in temporary quarters. There wasn't much to keep me busy except to clean our small area and care for my new baby. The four walls around me were confining and I had no way to escape to the mall or even to the grocery store. Even going out for a walk was limited since that January it rained every day . . . that is, except for the three days it snowed. I had been so excited to come, but it certainly wasn't what I had anticipated.

God used that time to help me learn to be content! If Paul could find contentment while hungry, find contentment in prison, and even be content while shipwrecked, perhaps there was hope for me. My situation wasn't a prison or a shipwreck, although it seemed as if there were some similarities.

This man of God said that he had learned contentment. It's probably the most important thing we can acquire. No matter how difficult your situation, if you quit looking at your problem you'll find someone else whose story is worse. Perhaps it is someone you can reach out to. You will find reasons to be thankful.

Too often we don't turn to God, until there's nowhere else to go. Whether you need wisdom, healing, or cash, it is amazing how the Lord provides for those who trust Him. There will be times when your faith will be stretched but God provides, perhaps with a check in the mail, or maybe with a better job. My home catering business provided leftovers that kept my refrigerator full. That business in turn opened up a position as director of food service for a small college. Reaching out to serve others, I found healing in the kitchen! Keeping busy with service, I was blessed.

Many years later, I look back upon God's goodness to me. Starting over was not easy, but it was so rewarding! He did supply all my needs and more! He's given me ministry, and opportunities I would never have imagined. "Give and it will be given unto you" is true. When you give, God gives back in incredible ways!

MOMENTS TO REFLECT:

Contentment needs to be learned, and often you must learn again. It is a process of acceptance. How do you allow God to help you become content in your situation?

MOMENTS TO REFRESH:

The contentment Paul speaks of is preceded by the peace that passes all understanding. Perhaps that is a good place to start.

MOMENTS TO REFOCUS:

In order to be anxious for nothing I must first take my requests to God with thanksgiving. I must also give my burden to Him and not pick it up again. Thank Him for your situation and for what will come out of it.

MOMENTS TO RESPOND:

Pray this: "Father, I bring my confusion, my pain, and my concern to You. Help me to look outside of my situation and see others through Your eyes. Help me to use the platform of understanding that You have given me to in turn minister to others."

Priscilla Wilson Taylor is the director of Women's Ministries for the Northern California/Nevada District of the Assemblies of God, a position she accepted in 1996. A graduate of Bethany College, she is currently completing a master of arts degree at Vanguard University.

For 22 years Priscilla and her husband pastored several churches. She taught Sunday School, Missionettes, and Women's Ministries. She contributed musically and assisted in the hospitality of the church.

It was in 1984 that Priscilla became "single again," and soon followed her two children to Bethany College when she became director of food service and conference director. She later was food service director at Bethel Church, San Jose.

Priscilla was ordained by the Assemblies of God in April 2002. Her professional skills include many years as secretary and in sales. She enjoys her catering business, "Angel Food," and recently published a cookbook, Priscilla's Kitchen.

Contact Priscilla Wilson Taylor at: ptaylor@agncn.org.

CHAPTER 33

His Work, My Health

Diane Tesch

*My flesh and my heart may fail; but God is the strength
of my heart and my portion forever.*
Psalm 73:26 (NASV)

Dr. Strick's words were firm and certain: "There is definitely something causing your daughter's right eye to protrude. Make an appointment immediately for a CT scan." The urgency in his voice frightened me. Leaving his office, we began 48 hours of uncertainty. Dread and anguish for our only child, 10-year-old Renee, engulfed me.

Waiting for test results we prayed, "Lord, help us to find out what it is . . . and calm our fears while we wait." I reminded myself that *God is not the author of fear.* Resolving to give Him my self-defeating thoughts and worries, my fears were quieted.

The diagnosis came. The protrusion was caused by a bone tumor called fibrous displasia. It grows most during rapid bone growth years. It is benign but disfiguring.

God gave us a quick answer to our earliest prayer . . . we knew *what* we were dealing with. Our prayers quickly changed to "God, please take away this mass and contour a normal eye socket again. But if You choose to do this another way, please walk through this with us. Lead us to the best possible surgeon. And, Lord, help us to come to understand what it is You want to do in us as a family—in Renee as she learns to live with adversity."

Little did I realize, these same prayers would be prayed twice more before Renee turned 16 and, again, for my own body later in life. God's Word reminds us, "Therefore do not be anxious for tomorrow; for tomorrow will care for itself. *Each* day has enough trouble of its own" (Matthew 6:34). Knowing I could rely on the Lord to carry this weight somehow allowed us to get through Renee's three surgeries in the next six years.

By the time we faced her third surgery, another whole facet of our life was developing. God's call on my husband's life was coming to fruition. When Wayne was 12, God gave him a vision for a network of camps for abused children that eventually became the nation's largest.

In 1985 the church where Wayne and I served as senior associate pastor launched the first Royal Family Kids' Camp under his direction. Thirty-seven of Orange County's severely abused children came. Knowing there were 1 million reported cases of abuse in the U.S. in 1985 quickly convinced us that the only way to make an impact was to enlist other churches to "go and do likewise."

By 1990, our church launched us to expand the ministry full-time to churches nationwide and, later, around the world. Overnight, Wayne began a travel schedule taking him away from home 200 nights a year. As director of operations, I managed the ministry from the back bedroom of our home.

Our passion for the "throwaway" kids of our society propelled us through the radical, exhausting change. We left job security and 1,500 people who had known us as family for 18 years. Our world had been turned upside down.

Faced with the insecurities of ministry start-up, raising support as district home missionaries, and creating a system for other churches to duplicate was stressful. Pioneering a ministry with no previous models was a walk of faith.

Keeping the pace of 14- to 16-hour days while Wayne traveled for two to three weeks at a time, and managing the household with the financial pressure of a growing ministry began to take its toll on my health.

One morning, I looked in the mirror and noticed large, ugly, red welts on my face. They were painful and would last four to six days, then subside. But the redness never went away. For the next two years, with medical help, I went through a trial-and-error elimination process while the condition worsened. As I asked God for healing, I heard myself repeating the prayer of 18 years earlier: "Lord, help me. Take it away. If that is not Your will, help me find out what it is, bring me good medical help, calm my fears and walk through this with me." His answer came not in the form of a miracle but in a dermatologist who identified the malady. I had lupus—the systemic form where the body attacks its own cells. Uncontrolled, it could develop into major organ damage to the heart, lungs, kidneys and brain.

There is no cure for lupus. Definite changes in my lifestyle had to be made if I was to continue by Wayne's side at Royal Family. Lifelong medication, frequent check-ups and extreme fatigue are ever-present companions, as are joint pain and potential retina damage.

I continue to pray, "God take this malady away." At the same time I believe God works through gifted medical professionals.

Learning to pace myself and live my life differently every day has become an ongoing challenge—not easy for a "type A personality" in a ministry the magnitude of Royal Family Kids' Camps. I must seek God's wisdom to know my limits and trust Him when I have reached them.

More than ever, talking with God has become the focus of my life. I ask Him for wisdom to reduce my stress. I have created a restful place in my home where quiet worship music brings a healing salve for my distressed body. I have changed my schedule to be in that quiet place daily, to seek God's direction and praise Him for the children's lives that are being changed.

What has God shown us with the health issues in our family? A 10-year-old girl, when faced with disfigurement, can claim 1 Chronicles 28:20, "Be strong and courageous," and He provides.

And even a strong-willed personality can change. To make the long distance-run, I must pace myself. A wild sprint, sustained and unbroken, will destroy even the best runner.

I've seen God walk with us through the unknowns and bring change and healing in *His* time. I have learned God is the strength of my heart, soul, mind and body. Now I do His work and trust Him with my health.

MOMENTS TO REFLECT:
Who, in my life, are the individuals who have experienced similar "unknowns" in their lives? When has God provided answers for me through other people? What friend could I call or meet with who would understand my current need?

MOMENTS TO REFRESH:
Read Psalm 41:1-3,11,12; Psalm 50:15; Psalm 62:2,7,8; Psalm 91:14,15; Isaiah 43:4; Isaiah 58:10-12; Matthew 6:31.

MOMENTS TO REFOCUS:
What are the prayers I've prayed more than once in my life—for myself; for others? Is there a common thread through those prayers that can build my faith? What dreams have I had for my life that I haven't pursued because I have been "too busy"?

MOMENTS TO RESPOND:
What are three simple steps I could take to bring about a change that God wants for me? Who might be blessed if these changes took place?

Diane Tesch is co-founder and director of operations and training for Royal Family Kids' Camps, Inc., the nation's leading network of camps specifically for abused children. More than 25,000 children have experienced a week at Royal Family since its founding in 1985. Royal Family received the Gold Award in 1990 from the Department of Social Services, Orange County, California, and the Kingsley Award from Christian Camping International in 1995.

In 2002, Diane was a Clara Barton Spectrum Award nominee for outstanding service to the needy of Orange County.

Diane is a speaker and co-author of Unlocking the Secret World: A Unique Ministry to Abused, Abandoned and Neglected Children and Moments Matter: The Stories of Royal Family Kids' Camps.

Diane and Wayne have been married for 36 years. They have one married daughter and two granddaughters.

Contact Diane Tesch (or learn more about Royal Family Kids' Camps) at: www.RFKC.org.

CHAPTER 34

"But You Said I Was Amazing"

Marjie Tourville

Pleasant words are a honeycomb, sweet to the soul and healing to the bones.
Proverbs 16:24 (NIV)

Josia, now 4 years old, is our oldest of four grandchildren. Visits to Mammaw and Poppop's house usually include jumping on our bed to see if he can touch the ceiling fan. Until recently, it was a challenge to jump that high, and when Josia reached the fan he heard lots of praise on how big he was getting and how amazingly high he could jump. This summer Mammaw had to change the rules of jumping for the fan as he is now tall enough to pull it off the ceiling. When I told Josia he could no longer jump for the fan, he replied, "But you said I was amazing." It really wasn't so much about reaching the fan, but more about hearing words of affirmation.

It has been said that people like you for how you make them feel. I'm sure all of us can reflect on someone who makes us feel special or identifies abilities and talents we possess. As a mom and Mammaw, it is easy for me to express that my children and grandchildren are smart and cute. Daniel Shaye, now 3 years old, has an incredible sense of humor. Kyle can charm a roomful of people even though he is only a year old. Lydia, just 3 months old, has stolen our hearts as the princess in our family. My parents are my best encouragers. They did and still do believe I can do anything that I try because I have God's creative power at work in my life to further His kingdom.

John 10:10 tells us that Jesus came to give us abundant life. When we accept Christ as Savior and Lord of our lives, it is exciting to know that the eternal life He provides for us doesn't begin when we die. God's gift of eternal life begins when we decide to follow Jesus. Eternal life is so much more than living forever. It is God's creative work within us accomplishing His work here on earth. A friend once gave me some good advice: If you see a need and feel unable to accomplish it, just ask the Creator of the universe to give you the creativity to know how to get it done. God was creative enough to put the universe in place; surely He is able to solve difficult challenges we face. Our words can help people identify the creative power of God working in their lives.

This week as you are interacting with your co-workers, friends, and family, ask yourself these four questions as a way of recognizing the gifts that God has given to the people around you. Then encourage them to develop their talents.

1. *Do I encourage those around me with kind words?* We all do an adequate job at telling ourselves that we can't do things or we aren't smart enough. Many times that is only a defense mechanism to protect ourselves from the possibility of not succeeding. Your words of encouragement may be the very thing a person needs to overcome fear and a lack of self-confidence.

2. *Do I make those near me feel special?* A cutting sense of humor is never funny. I am acquainted with a man who jokes about his wife's cooking. I often wonder how that must hurt her confidence. I am so thankful for a loving husband who encourages me whether I prepare a feast or "burnt offering." His tender words are a safe place for me when I feel vulnerable. No one ever gets tired of hearing that they're doing a good job.

3. *Do I help mend broken dreams?* Our world is full of people who are ready to reject ideas that are not "inside their box." If we are ever going to achieve something outstanding, there will probably be repeated failures before the idea is perfected. Look for someone this week who has failed in an attempt for something out of the ordinary. Speak words of encouragement and confidence in their ability to see the idea through to completion. We can encourage one another to dream the impossible because we serve the God of the impossible.

4. *Do I challenge those around me to be the best they can be?* It is not nearly so important to do things perfectly as it is to give your best effort. I'm so thankful for people who keep giving me a second chance when I don't complete something up to their ability—just my ability.

The way we communicate with those around us is important. What an awesome opportunity we have to make a difference in the lives of those closest to us. We can be instruments of blessing just by speaking words of affirmation and recognizing the hand of God at work in their lives. There is a wealth of talent just waiting to be discovered and developed. Words can surely be healing to our bones when spoken with love and encouragement.

MOMENTS TO REFLECT:
Who has made a difference in your life with their words?

MOMENTS TO REFRESH:
God's eternal life is at work in you.

MOMENTS TO REFOCUS:
You can make a difference in someone's future by your words.

MOMENTS TO RESPOND:
Ask God to show you who needs to be encouraged.

Marjie Tourville lives near Harrisburg, Pennsylvania, and is the wife of Stephen R. Tourville, superintendent of the Pennsylvania-Delaware District of the Assemblies of God. Steve and Marjie pastored in Pennsylvania for 25 years, then moved to the district office as Home Missions director for the district. In Springfield, Missouri, Marjie was the administrative assistant to the president of Convoy of Hope while

Steve served as the Intercultural Ministries director for Assemblies of God U.S. Missions.

Marjie earned a B.A. in organizational management from Eastern University and also attended Valley Forge Christian College. She is currently studying with the Institute of Pastoral Counseling associated with EMERGE Ministries.

Marjie's administrative and computer software skills were important aspects of her extensive experience in the corporate world. Organizing and leading ministries, and speaking and training various groups have given outlet to her passion to prepare believers to serve the Lord.

Steve and Marjie have two children and four grandchildren.

Contact Marjie Tourville at: Marjietourville@aol.com.

What Do You See?

Rhonda Trask

When Joseph woke up, he did what the angel of the Lord had commanded him and took Mary home as his wife.
Matthew 1:24 (NIV)

Sight is a very interesting sense. People often have differences of opinion depending upon the angle from which they view an object or situation. The complexity of sight is illustrated well by the optical illusion. An optical illusion occurs when someone sees one of two images, but not both images simultaneously.

During team-building activities, I have frequently heard people encouraging team members who are struggling to see one or both images. "Tilt your head to the right." "Focus on the left corner." Inevitably, as an individual follows the verbal and visual cues from a teammate the optical illusion dissipates, revealing imagery that was previously undetected.

Consider the optical illusion in the light of our personal walk with Jesus Christ. As we endeavor to follow Christ and ascertain the plans He has for our lives, we must be careful. Much like one can overlook the dual imagery of an optical illusion, we can easily miss the multiplicity of life experiences that seem simple at first glance. Perhaps you are like me and have been guilty of moving ahead too quickly after identifying only one aspect of the picture instead of its entirety. How thankful I am for the Holy Spirit who, like a teammate, provides cues that assist me in seeing more clearly the totality of life's experiences.

Spiritual eyesight impacts one's speech, actions, and faith. Because of this, assessing our spiritual eyesight is just as important as having our physical eyesight tested. There is a basic assessment tool by which we can examine the condition of our spiritual eyesight. The tool is composed of three steps: recognition, realization, and revelation. We can draw important lessons from the life of Joseph, earthly father of Jesus, to help us comprehend the challenge of seeing life's daily scenarios through spiritually fit eyes.

RECOGNITION

In the Gospel of Matthew, we see that God administered a spiritual eye exam to Joseph. Mary, his fiancée, was pregnant and he was not the father. Joseph recognized there was a predicament. In response to this situation he devised a plan that he believed would best serve Mary and himself. Since he "did not want to expose her to public disgrace, he had in mind to divorce her quietly" (Matthew 1:19).

However well-intentioned Joseph's response was, God desired to show Joseph that the recognition level on which he was operating was limited. So God tested Joseph's spiritual eyesight through a dream and the words of an angel: "Joseph son of David, do not be afraid to take Mary home as your wife, because what is conceived in her is from the Holy Spirit" (Matthew 1:20).

REALIZATION

After Joseph awoke from the dream, the second phase of his spiritual eyesight exam was administered. Passing the realization test required that Joseph abandon his assessment and man-made plans concerning Mary. He was challenged to view the scenario with eyes that focused on God's goals and purposes and not his own. As Joseph reflected upon the words spoken to him by the angel, he realized that his initial response to the situation had been in error. The Bible tells us that Joseph awoke and took Mary home as his wife (Matthew 1:24). Joseph realized that the unborn Baby Mary was carrying was God's Son. This demonstrated improvement in his spiritual eyesight—realization of the true picture.

REVELATION

Next, Joseph's spiritual eyesight would be tested in the third area, the realm of revelation. While realization required Joseph to reevaluate his initial reaction and response to an unexpected scenario, revelation demanded a lifestyle of subjection to God's perspective in every scenario. Returning to Matthew's Gospel, we see Joseph demonstrate exceptional perception in the area of revelation. On three separate occasions Joseph received revelation regarding dangers that threatened the life of Jesus, and each time, without hesitation, he obeyed the voice of God without thought for his own needs.

This same three-pronged spiritual eye exam can be administered to our own lives. Like Joseph, the individual who desires to see what God sees must be willing to deny her own goals and perspective. She must withstand the scrutiny of those who question choices due to their inability to see the full picture—the dual imagery that spiritual eyes of revelation see.

Being misunderstood by those around us is difficult. Are we willing to become like Joseph and see life through eyes of revelation regardless of the sacrifice involved? Do our lives emulate Joseph's example, or do we move rapidly through life relying on our natural eyesight versus the spiritual eyesight that God desires us to possess? How incredible that a Jewish carpenter, over 2,000 years ago, helped to change the course of the world because he allowed God to show him the dual imagery contained within a seemingly one-dimensional image. What might God be trying to show us? It all begins with what we see.

MOMENTS TO REFLECT:
Assess your spiritual eyesight. Which of the three categories best describes how you view life on a regular basis (recognition, realization, and/or revelation)?

MOMENTS TO REFRESH:
God desires to help you see the dual imagery contained within the events and/or challenges of life, just as He assisted Joseph.

MOMENTS TO REFOCUS:

Understand that in order to see beyond the level of recognition (natural eyesight) you should:

1. Assess your initial response to a situation.

2. Ask the Holy Spirit to provide cues to help you realize the broader implications that could be involved in a situation.

3. Acknowledge that revelation will come as you live in obedience to the cues the Holy Spirit will provide.

MOMENTS TO RESPOND:

"Lord, help me to emulate Joseph's lifestyle of obedience with eyes of revelation. Let Your will be accomplished as my eyes are focused on Your plans and not my own."

Rhonda Trask and her husband, Bradley, pastor Brighton Assembly of God located in Brighton, Michigan, a church they pioneered in 1992. During the church's first seven years, Rhonda oversaw the children's and Christian education areas of ministry while teaching full-time in the Farmington Public School System. In 1999, she left the public schools to serve full-time at the church as the director of Revolution Student Ministries and Christian Education. Currently, she leads these two areas as well as DIAG Ministries (young adults) and 2/42 Groups (adult cell groups).

Rhonda's educational degrees include a B.A., teaching certificate, and master's degree, earned from Michigan State University, Madonna University, and Wayne State University. She is pursuing a specialist's degree in the field of educational leadership and curriculum development.

Contact Rhonda Trask at: Rhonda@brightonag.org.

CHAPTER 36

Blessed Are the Tears

Kay Zello

In the day when I cried out, You answered me,
and made me bold with strength in my soul.
Psalm 138:3 (NKJV)

I am 27 years old, happily married and the mother of three. But I am utterly alone in a hospital bed on the 13th floor of the Pollack Hospital for Chest Diseases. Iron bars on the window cast shadows on the opposite wall of my clinically barren room. Left over from the early 20th century, they are sober reminders of an era when hopeless tuberculosis patients chose a jump to certain death rather than face future years locked up and wasting away. I cannot accept the bars but come to understand them. Days are eternally long and every night is an endless dark valley stretching from sundown to dawn. My clammy flesh is cold, then burns with raging fever. Nurses are angels of mercy, but they are in short supply and seem vastly out-numbered by nocturnal demons invisibly roaming the hall-ways at will. Unsolicited they sneak into my room, magni-fying pain and loneliness, whispering despair, breathing in my face the horrible stench of fear. Silently a tear rolls from the corner of my eye, trickles down my cheek, and drops into my ear.

Through the gray darkness my fingers grope the night-stand feeling for the familiar soft leather of my Bible. Too sick to read, I hug it tightly to my weary chest and plead for God's mercy. Slowly, I feel the focus shifting from my frail body, consumed by tuberculosis and exhausted by an unceasing cough, to my soul crying out for help. God has my full attention now. I am stripped of alternatives. "Busy taking care of baby and toddlers and a dear pastor hus-band who needs my help, important things demand my time, I will catch up with You later, Lord." All excuses are gone. The narrow bed of my confinement has become a trysting place for the lover of my soul. He comes gently and my mournful groaning fades, giving way to a sweet song in the night. "He's all I need. He's all I need. Jesus is all I need." My body is weak and so tired, but strength enters my soul. Jesus is with me, and He is enough.

One day my husband brings our children to the hospi-tal. A pair of pretty little girls—Kathleen is 4 and Bonnie is not quite 2—and Michael, who is 3. My mother-in-law is holding their hands in a small patch of grass directly beneath my window. My husband supports me as I clutch a pair of binoculars and peer down between the iron bars. Little hands are waving and blowing me kisses. I smile and return the love signals. Brimming tears tumble from my eyes into the rim of the binoculars. "O God, how is this to be borne?"

Then I remember my last night at home in our apartment attached to the back of the church. There is no narthex. Open the door in our living room and you are in the holy sanctuary. Our children share a small bedroom, two toddlers stacked in bunk beds and one still in a crib. My worried husband has finally succumbed to a fitful sleep, and I slip from our bed into the children's room. Silently I walk to each of them, lightly touching their tousled heads. Tear-choked, my prayer is desperate. "God, how can I leave my babies? The doctor said it would be months, perhaps a year." I struggle against a mounting fear. "I won't be here when they need me!" God heard my cry and He answered clearly and distinctly: *Kay, I will take better care of them than if you were here.*

People have asked how I know God's voice. My standard answer is that He says what no one else is likely to say and what I could not think up. Who else but God would boldly say, "I will take better care of your children than you can"? Not even my husband who is a wonderful father would say that to me. Their grandmother who loves them dearly would not say it. But God did and I believed Him.

Looking through binocular lenses blurred with tears, I remember His words, and once again strength enters my soul.

Blessed are the tears that fall
That clean the windows of the soul
And usher in a change of heart
And bring a joy that angels know

Blessed are the tears that fall.

—Bryan Duncan

Over a period of several months, God miraculously healed my disease-ravaged lungs. I was released from the hospital, and three years later gave birth to another son, Timothy. That was 32 years ago. Our four children have grown up loving and serving God and have made me the joyful grandmother of 11 grandchildren.

MOMENTS TO REFLECT:
When I cried out to God, He answered. God did not change the outer circumstances, but He changed the inner me. He gave me soul strength.

MOMENTS TO REFRESH:
You and I can trust God to take care of what is dear to us. The last verse of Psalm 138 says, "The Lord will perfect *that which* concerns me."

MOMENTS TO REFOCUS:
God is concerned about your body and good health, but He cares much more for your eternal soul and your relationship with Him.

MOMENTS TO RESPOND:

Don't be ashamed of your tears. They are often the most honest expression of your deepest need. Your hurts touch God's heart. Ask God to fill your loneliness with himself and replace worry and fear with quietness and confidence.

Kay Zello is an ordained minister with the Assemblies of God. She served as an associate pastor for 17 years and is a skilled teacher and preacher. For many years she taught a Bible class for inner-city women in Washington, D.C. She has been the featured speaker at retreats and conferences across America and in 15 countries, including Pakistan, Poland, Lithuania, and South Africa. Kay has been married to Mike Zello, also an ordained minister, for 42 years. She and her husband are presently Assemblies of God world missionaries with Global Teen Challenge. (Kay began working with Teen Challenge in Brooklyn, New York, under founder and director David Wilkerson. Her maiden name, Kay Ware, is mentioned in The Cross and the Switchblade *book, which has sold more than 26 million copies.)*

When they are not overseas Kay and her husband live in Locust Grove, Virginia. They have 4 grown children and 11 grandchildren.

Contact Kay Zello at: kayzello@cs.com.

ENDNOTES

Chapter 1

1. *Young's Analytical Concordance* (Grand Rapids: Wm. B. Eerdmans Publishing Company, 1969), 811.

Chapter 7

1. D. Martyn Lloyd-Jones, *Spiritual Depression: Its Causes and Cure* (Grand Rapids: Wm. B. Eerdmans Publishing Company, 1965), 194,195.
2. Charles R. Swindoll, *Growing Strong in the Seasons of Life* (Portland, OR: Multnomah Press, 1983), 136.

Chapter 8

1. *Eerdman's Bible Commentary* (Grand Rapids: Wm. B. Eerdmans Publishing Company), 54.
2. *Eerdman's Bible Commentary*, 53,54.
3. *The Sacramento Bee*, May 24, 2003.

Chapter 18

1. J. Oswald Sanders, *Enjoying Intimacy with God* (Chicago: Moody Press, 1980), 12.
2. "Designed for Desire," http://www.growthtrac.com/discover/cb932/point2.shtml.
3. C.S. Lewis, *The Weight of Glory* (San Francisco: Harper, 2001), 1,2.

Chapter 25

1. Benjamin Spock, *Baby and Child Care* (New York: Pocket Books, 1992), 487 (paraphrase).
2. Cited in Robert Strand, *Mini Moments for Fathers* (Green Forest, AR: New Leaf Press, 1995), 18.
3. David A. Seamands, *Healing for Damaged Emotions* (Colorado Springs, CO: Victor Publishing, 2002), 48 (paraphrase).

Chapter 29

1. Thomas O. Chisholm, 1866-1960
   Copyright 1923
   Renewal 1951 by Hope Publishing Company
   Carol Stream, IL 60188

Peggy Horn, Huldah Buntain and Lillian Sparks (from left)

Peggy Horn is the national outreach coordinator for Convoy of Hope, an international compassion ministry. She participates in Convoy outreaches as a team member in the United States and abroad, speaks at churches, and trains volunteers.

Peggy and her husband, Ken, pastored churches in California and Oregon before moving to Springfield, Missouri, where Ken is managing editor of *Today's Pentecostal Evangel*. Peggy has had longstanding involvement in Women's Ministries on local and sectional levels. She worked with Missionettes programs, and co-authored a manual for the former Missionettes badge program.

Before marriage Peggy did resident ministry in a Christian orphanage in Mexico. She traveled widely throughout Europe with her husband in the 1980s, ministering behind the Iron Curtain and also in Western Europe where she has also ministered recently.

Peggy's administrative and organizational skills have been utilized in churches and the secular field. She is a regular volunteer with Tax Counseling Services for the Elderly of the Southwest Missouri Office on Aging.

Peggy lives in Springfield, Missouri.

Lillian Sparks is the former national director of the Assemblies of God Women's Ministries Department, where she coordinated the denomination's Women's Ministries program, which involved more than 400,000 women and girls. In addition to her administrative responsibilities, Sparks was editor of *Woman's Touch*, an award-winning bimonthly magazine.

Lillian is one of three daughters born to parents who began planting churches in the early 1950s and, although retired, are still involved in visitation and teaching in their local church. An ordained minister with the Pennsylvania-Delaware District, Sparks holds a B.A. in biblical literature from Northwest College of the Assemblies of God in Kirkland, Washington, and a diploma in sacred music from Zion Bible Institute. During the past 30 years, she has ministered in some 45 states, numerous foreign countries, and to hundreds of congregation. She served as Pennsylvania-Delaware District Women's Ministries director for two years. Most recently Lillian worked with World-Serve.

Lillian has filled the shoes of pastor's wife, Christian education director, college music professor, kindergarten teacher, and retreat and seminar speaker.

Sparks is the author of *Tough Cookie* and *Parents Cry Too*. Both tell the story of her eldest son, Bryon, and his lifelong battle with a rare skin disease. Bryon went to be with the Lord in 1995 at the age of 21. Lillian and her husband, Rev. Stephen Sparks, have three children: Leann, Jenell, and Brent. They all reside in Springfield, Missouri.

For a complete list of books
offered by Onward Books, Inc.
and an order form, please call or write:

Onward Books, Inc.
4848 South Landon Court
Springfield, MO 65810
417-890-7465

e-mail address:
onwardbooks@aol.com

Or visit our Web site at:
www.onwardbooks.com

NOTES

NOTES

NOTES

NOTES

NOTES

NOTES